ASTON MARTIN
1914 to 1940
a pictorial review

by

Inman Hunter

TRANSPORT BOOKMAN PUBLICATIONS

©1976   Transport Bookman Publications
Syon Park, Brentford
London TW8 8JF

ISBN 0 85184 020 5

Cover design by
David Harris

Designed and typeset by
Barbara Harris

IBM Baskerville 11 on 13

Printed in England by
HGA Printing Company Limited, Brentford

CONTENTS

Part III - 1936 - 1940 - Gordon Sutherland and the 2 litres

Appendix I

Appendix II

To 'Bert' and Vera

AUTHOR'S FOREWORD

One day in October 1929 at the Olympia Motor Show the Chief
Mechanical Engineer of the British Thomson-Houston Company,
one time designer of the Adams and Cheswold cars, stood against
the rail enclosing the exhibits of the small specialist firm of Aston
Martin Motors Ltd. By his side was his schoolboy son to whom,
with professional appreciation, he indicated the splendid engineering embodied in the stripped Aston Martin chassis. That schoolboy
was the writer.

Twelve months later in defiance of a long standing paternal plot
for me to join the Austin Motor Company I was an apprentice with
Aston Martin working as fitter's mate on the assembly of the 1931
work's racers. Today one of those team cars stands in my garage,
my most prized possession.

Thus started a life long love affair with the Aston Martin and
from it arose the inspiration for this volume. However, such a
splendid collection of illustrations would have been impossible
without the most generous co-operation of officials and members
of the Aston Martin Owners Club, magazine proprietors and
editorial staff, the National Motor Museum and individual enthusiasts several of whom opened their valuable personal scrap books
giving me free choice of their rare pictures. For this reason the
original source or photographer is not always known and I hasten
to ask forgiveness should I have inadvertently infringed anyone's
copyright.

Wherever possible pictures have been selected that might best
illustrate particular points made in the text and for that reason
the photographic quality tends to vary considerably. In some

Happy reunion! The author who was an apprentice at Aston Martin in the early 1930's with his 1931 team car and former master, A.C. Bertelli then in his 80th year.

cases the only available illustrations were snap shots and news cuttings but it was thought preferable to use comparatively imperfect pictures rather than none at all. It has also been my aim to use non-action pictures when possible for this is not a racing history of the Aston Martin. Fred and Ellis and myself covered this side of the story pretty thoroughly some years ago in *Aston Martin, the story of a sports car* (Motor Racing Publications Ltd., 1957). For the commentary on each individual model I have relied to a great extent on personal memory augmented by consulting contemporary journals, *The Autocar, Motor Sport, The Motor* and the sadly defunct *Light Car* and *The Auto*. The background story of the three phases of the Company's pre-war history was prepared from talks with Lionel Martin shortly before he died, the late Lord Charnwood (The Hon: John Benson), my good friends Bert and Vera Bertelli and by way of extensive correspondence with R. Gordon Sutherland.

Whilst the immediate source of each picture is given individual acknowledgement I am also greatly indebted to many people for their kindness in replying to my inquiring letters and for assistance in various other ways. These include the proprietors of *Motor Sport* for permission to quote from their issue of June 1930, L'Automobile-Club de L'Ouest, D.W. Aylett, Chairman of the Aston Martin Owners Club together with members and officials of that association, D.C. Bridle whose father was works photographer at Feltham, John Classey, A.P. Demaus, F.E. Ellis, Adrian Feather, Keith Fletcher, who, as an antiquarian bookseller, came up with a pre-war work's scrap book, Anthony Harding, Malcolm Hardy, A.P. Hartwell, Nigel P. Hewin, the Public Relations Officer of Coventry Climax Engines Ltd, C.I. Henty, Brian Joscelyne, Editor of *A.M.*, the official organ of the Owners Club, Ian MacGregor, Neil Murray, J.A.M. Patrick and Ray and Joan Stokes who with overwhelming kindness entertained the Bertellis and ourselves at so many dinner parties in their home.

That the book has appeared at all and in such an attractive form I am indebted to my publisher Frank Stroud and his colleagues

Peter Malcolmson, Barbara and David Harris. And, last but not least, I am indebted to Wilhelm Staudinger who performed a small miracle in tracing the present whereabouts of the German pre-war racing driver Werner Hillegaart.

To all these people and those who helped them to help me I tender a very warm Thank You.

Whitton, 1976

PICTURE CREDITS

The Author is pleased to acknowledge with gratitude that the photographs appearing in this book have kindly been provided as under:

Aston Martin Owners Club: pp. 43 (top), 81 (top), 89 (bottom), 109 (bottom), 119, 121, 125 (top), 135 (top), 137 (top), 167 (top), 175 (bottom), 192. Autocar: pp. 29, 46 (top), 48 (top), 62 (bottom), 64, 73, 77 (bottom), 79, 83 (bottom), 85 (top), 91 (top), 97 (bottom), 101 (bottom), 105 (bottom), 109 (top), 111 (bottom), 113, 123 (bottom), 133 (top), 137 (bottom), 141 (bottom), 159, 165, 173 (top). T.F. Bailey: pp. 171 (top). A.C. Bertelli: pp. 62 (top). C.I.H. Black: pp. 107 (bottom). Tony Byles: pp. 77 (top), 127 (top). J. Cheyne: pp. 46 (centre). P.N. Delves-Broughton: pp. 47 (bottom), 131 (bottom). F.E. Ellis: pp. 17, 31 (bottom), 35, 37, 39 (bottom), 41 (bottom), 45, 48 (bottom), 49 (bottom). J.B. Emmott: pp. 71, 129 (top). P. Engerbach: pp. 163. A.F. Rivers Fletcher: pp. 85 (bottom). D. Gay: pp. 103 (top). J. Goodall: pp. 51. Miss Betty Haig: 119 (top). Claude Hill: pp. 161 (bottom), 171 (bottom). W. Hillegaart: pp. 135 (centre & bottom). W.S. Jackson: pp. 119 (centre). T.A.S.O. Mathieson: pp. 39 (top). Motor Sport: pp. 115 (bottom). National Motor Museum: pp 93 (bottom), 95 (bottom), 141 (top). Old Motor: pp. 14, 55. H. Oosterbaan: pp. 99 (bottom). Photo Lafay: pp. 101 (top), 117. Cyril Posthumus: pp. 56. Radio Times Hulton Picture Library: pp. 89 (top). Ralph Stein: pp. 161 (top). Ray Stokes: pp. 8. R. Gordon Sutherland: pp. 148, 169 (bottom), 177 (top). J. Trentham: pp. 105 (top). E.J. Warburton: pp. 27 (bottom), 49 (top). Capt. The Rev. Herbert Ward: pp. 47 (top), 49 (top). All others are from the author's collection.

ASTON-MARTIN or ASTON MARTIN?

When in 1914 the late Lionel Martin decided to enter the light car market with a car of his own conception he named it the Aston-Martin, spelling it with a hyphen and thus it was known up to 1926 when his company Messrs Bamford and Martin Ltd went into liquidation.

A new company Messrs Aston Martin Motors Ltd then took over and dropped the hyphen calling their new cars Aston Martins. But by 1930, by which time the firm had become Aston Martin Ltd, the hyphen crept back into some of the firm's advertising. From then on they were quite indecisive, even their catalogues varied from year to year and in adopting a new enamel badge in 1932 they firmly re-established the hyphenated spelling on the radiators of their cars whilst still unable to make up their minds in print .... the famous *Ulster* was an Aston-Martin in the catalogue whereas the standard Mark II models were Aston Martins!

After the war David Brown on acquiring the company dropped the hyphen completely (although adding his own name as a prefix) and today, two proprietary companies later, the marque is once more just plain Aston Martin and so for the sake of consistency it will be thus spelt throughout this book.

PART I

1914 - 1925

LIONEL MARTIN'S ASTONS

The late Lionel Martin at the wheel of the special Singer he evolved for competition use before the introduction of his Aston Martin car in 1914.

INTRODUCTION

The first Aston Martin, built in 1914, was an Aston Martin in name only for beneath its rather cumbersome body was an Isotta-Fraschini chassis originally built for the 1908 *Grand Prix des Voiturettes*, its engine replaced by the latest offering from Coventry-Simplex, a 1400 cc four cylinder side valve unit.

This hybrid special made its first public appearance in the *M.C.C. Brighton Trial* of 1914 just a few weeks before the outbreak of war and for the first time was referred to in the press as an Aston Martin. It was the personal creation of a well known sporting motorist Lionel Martin whose family fortunes accrued from some tin mines in Cornwall and a group of Lincolnshire quarries. These enterprises did not excite Lionel Martin overmuch, so leaving them in the hands of able management he devoted his energies to the running of a small garage in London's Fulham Road in which he was joined by a partner named Robert Bamford who having served his apprenticeship at the Teddington Launch Works of Messrs Hesse and Savory was a practical engineer. Unlike his partner Lionel Martin had no engineering training whatsoever but was an experienced motorist, in the days when motoring meant more than being able to drive a car. As a connoisseur of fine cars he had an uncanny knack of sensing what was right in design and construction. In particular he had an eye for quality and detail aspects of design. After the war when the Aston Martin reached a production stage it became renowned for its high standard of workmanship and fine detail work.

That the car was very much Martin's own personal creation is suggested by the fact that its name did not incorporate that of Bamford but of the hill at Aston Clinton where Martin had been successful at the wheel of a tuned 10 hp Singer.

In 1913 the partnership became a limited company, Messrs Bamford and Martin Ltd, and was operating from premises at Henniker Place in South Kensington, workshops which had previously been the London depot of Hesse and Savory where Robert Bamford had been manager after completing his apprentice-ship at Teddington. Apart from the business of general motor repairers, Bamford and Martin held an agency for Singer cars, rather sedate and practical vehicles which by no stretch of imagi-nation could be described as sporting. But this did not deter Lionel Martin in his efforts to run a Singer in competition. With the aid of his works foreman, Jack Addis, he gradually transformed a mundane 10 hp Singer with a maximum speed of some 40 mph into a 70 mph sports car which did extremely well in trials and hill climbs with the result that the little Kensington firm began to receive requests for replicas.

Tempting as these enquiries were, extensive tuning of further Singers was not considered a practical proposition as Lionel Martin's special was very much a one-off job with hundreds of costly hours of labour behind it. However Martin was prompted to think in terms of a completely original car which would reflect his vast experience as a practical motorist and would incorporate many of his own personal fads and fancies. He claimed to have in mind what he described as an 'English Bugatti' and in many respects his ultimate productions fell little short of this ideal.

The design laid down in the summer of 1914 incorporated a newly introduced 1400 cc Coventry-Simplex engine with gearbox and transmission to Martin's specification made by the Birmingham firm of E.G. Wrigley and Co.. The frame was of conventional design with semi-elliptic front springs and three quarter elliptics at the rear.

Whilst awaiting delivery of the specially designed components, Martin installed one of the Coventry-Simplex engines in the six

A side valve saloon outside the Abingdon Road works of Bamford and Martin Ltd off Kensington High Street.

A Record!

On Wednesday, February 15th, 1922,
an *Aston-Martin Light Car*
tuned and driven by Mr. H. Kensington
Moir, broke the Brooklands Test Hill
Record in 9·29 seconds.

The average speed, from a standing start,
for the 117 yards of an average gradient
of 1 in 5·02 was 25·85 miles per hour.

We wish to express our thanks to:—
The ZENITH CARBURETTER COMPANY, LTD.
The FELLOWS MAGNETO COMPANY, LTD.
The ROBINHOOD ENGINEERING WORKS, LTD.
(K.L.G. Plugs.)
The ANGLO-AMERICAN OIL COMPANY, LTD.
whose Accessories contributed to the above success.

The car which accomplished this performance had not been altered, adjusted, or even
the engine decarbonized in 2,500 miles previous running, including the Junior Car
Club's 200 Mile Race.

Bamford & Martin, Limited,
53, Abingdon Road, KENSINGTON,
LONDON, W.8.

One of the earliest Aston Martin advertisements featured Bunny's
successful attack on the Brooklands test hill record.

year old Isotta-Fraschini chassis and the first car to bear the name Aston Martin came into being but almost immediately Europe was at war and the project had to be abandoned for the duration. Robert Bamford being a reservist was called up into the Army Service Corps and Lionel Martin went to the Admiralty. The little mews workshops were shut down and its small collection of machine tools handed over to the Sopwith aviation company at Kingston-on-Thames where Jack Addis became transport manager. As for the Isotta hybrid, Martin used this throughout the war years and it was still active in competition two or three years after the armistice.

When hostilities were over Robert Bamford, who had never had much enthusiasm for the Aston Martin project sold his share in the partnership to Martin whose wife Katherine became co-director giving the couple sole control of the firm which re-commenced operations at 53 Abingdon Road off Kensington High Street. The war time demand for tin having swollen his family fortunes Lionel Martin, as enthusiastic as ever, somewhat extravagantly devoted a considerable portion of his resources to resuming his plans for car production. In furthering his plans he had the vital engineering experience of Jack Addis who had rejoined his old boss and was to remain with him until the firm's demise in 1925 when he emigrated to New Zealand.

In designing his new car Martin worked closely with an ex-Coventry-Simplex draughtsman named Robb who had been involved in laying out the engine used in the Isotta-Fraschini hybrid before the war.

Robb's first assignment was to design a new engine which would be exclusive to the Aston Martin. Basically it was similar to the prototype but with a bore and stroke of 66½ mm x 107 mm, giving a capacity of 1487 cc. Three new chassis were built up with the new engine but in the course of testing the first car the frame fractured behind the rear gearbox mounting. The design was suitably modified and a further prototype built which apart from its Sankey wheels and brakes on the rear wheels only was in most aspects the chassis that eventually went into production.

Meanwhile Addis assembled a special short wheelbase racing car which for no known reason was called *Bunny* and whose racing and record successes were to become almost legendary. Martin however sought more power than that developed by the efficient little side valve engine and Robb drew up a single overhead camshaft unit with sixteen valves but its performance was disappointing when tried in a special track racer and it was not proceded with. However the late Count Louis Zborowski who had driven the car was very impressed with the A.M. chassis and financed the building of a new sixteen valve twin overhead camshaft engine based on the straight eight Grand Prix Ballot. Using this engine two extremely handsome little cars were built and run in the *French Grand Prix* of 1922 at Strasbourg in which they were driven by Zborowski and the late Clive Gallop. Both cars retired on this their first outing but the twin cam engine was ultimately most successful and several examples were built and used in both cars and racing boats. However, exciting as these competition activities must have been to all concerned, they were taxing the firm's resources to the full and the marque seemed little nearer to the production stage. Furthermore despite Zborowski's alleged £10,000 outlay on the Grand Prix cars, Lionel Martin himself was spending a small fortune with little or no financial return. A.C. Bertelli has estimated that the whole Aston Martin project cost Lionel Martin between £100,000 and £150,000!

Eventually common sense prevailed and in 1923 a firm sales drive was instigated and Malcolm Campbell who had showrooms at 27 Albemarle Street was appointed London agent. Whilst in appearance some of the prototype Astons had displayed a certain crudity and 'home made' appearance the production models were beautifully engineered and usually very handsome particularly when fitted with the rare small G.P. radiatior.

With a staff which at the most totalled perhaps twenty or so fitters it is remarkable how many cars were built and sold in the three years leading up to the company's collapse in 1925. Well over

The cylinder block of the standard side valve engine.

The crankcase showing the stiff webbed bearer arms.

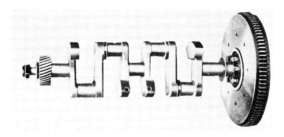

The three bearing crankshaft.

BAMFORD & MARTIN, LIMITED.

ENGINEERS.

TELEPHONE WESTERN 4003.
TELEGRAMS ASTOMARTIA, KENS, LONDON.

MANUFACTURERS OF
THE ASTON-MARTIN CAR.

53, ABINGDON ROAD,
KENSINGTON,
LONDON, W.8.

Kenneth W. Crabb, Esq.,   5th March. 1925.
"Mauderlea",
Lundin Links,
Fifeshire.

Dear Sir,

        We are obliged for your letter of yesterday's date and have pleasure in enclosing Catalogue of Aston Martin Cars.

        The gear ratios are 4.0, 5.2, 7.4 and 14.1.

        The Overhead valve engine, which though standardized we only build to special order is 65 x 112 m.m.

        We strongly recommend for anything but strenuous racing our side valve 66.5 x 107 m.m. engine with which practically all our successes have been achieved.

        Not only is it absolutely docile and reliable, but it is capable of very high speeds: last year in the 200 Miles race a private owner with a standard touring car finished at a average of 79.5 and the year before, another private owner with a standard sports car averaged 86.6.

        We can confidently state that no other standard car with engine of similar size whether side valve or overhead has ever done these speeds in the hands of a private owner.

        Yours faithfully,

FOR AND ON BEHALF OF
BAMFORD & MARTIN LTD.

Lionel Martin.
DIRECTOR.

CARS DRIVEN ONLY AT CLIENTS' OWN RISK AND RESPONSIBILITY.

Addressed to a prospective client, this letter was written shortly before the demise of the original company.

fifty cars were produced in that period and yet at the same time Lionel Martin, at least initially, managed to continue the firm's competition activities unabated. The Grand Prix cars, the track cars and *Bunny*, all were active most weekends throughout the country, often with amateur drivers at the wheel but mostly with full works support. Side valve and twin cam engines were swopped from car to car in a frenzy of activity, and this, combined with registration plates being freely exchanged, makes the early racing history of the Aston Martin a formidable task to sort out. However it is certain that the Aston Martin was building up a tremendous reputation further enchanced when it became the first light car to take world records. In May 1921 at Brooklands, *Bunny* covered no less than 12,000 miles in 16 hours at an average speed of 67.12 mph. Then came *Razor Blade*, a very narrow single seater conceived with the express purpose of covering 100 miles in 1 hour. In this it was not successful although later it was raced with a fair measure of success by a number of drivers.

By 1924 Lionel Martin had stretched his financial resources to the limit and he had no alternative but to seek outside assistance and it fell to the Charnwood family to give the firm a fresh lease of life. In July of that year Lady Dorothy Charnwood acquired the assets of the company and a new board of directors was formed consisting of Lionel Martin, Katherine Martin, George Eustace Ridley Shield and Lady Charnwood's son the Hon John Roby Benson. The latter had just taken a degree in engineering at Oxford and with great enthusiasm designed a new twin overhead camshaft eight valve engine which due to a string of misfortunes was never raced as intended but formed part of the firm's first appearance at the London Motor Show in October 1925. It was also their swan song. Time had run out for Bamford and Martin Ltd. In retrospect it would appear that too much money had been spent on racing in the early years and when they came to settle down to serious production their facilities proved inadequate, their product too expensive and available finance insufficient to allow expansion and so reduce costs.

A couple of weeks after the Motor Show, a receiver was appointed and Lionel Martin departed to the family quarries. The receiver discussed several propositions put forward by various companies including Vauxhall Motors, the Bristol Aeroplane Company and the French motor manufacturers, Donnet et Zedel, but their talks came to nothing and eventually it was the Charnwoods who got together with Messrs Renwick and Bertelli Ltd, a small Birmingham firm of consulting and development engineers and the Aston Martin car was launched into a second lease of life. Lionel Martin retained an active interest in motor sport and for many years was an RAC official. He died in 1945 after being involved in an accident on his pedal tricycle. A sad end to a great enthusiast whose dreams did not quite reach the fulfillment they deserved.

An unsolved mystery

THE FIRST ASTON MARTIN?

As we have seen the first car to bear the name Aston Martin was a hybrid special consisting of an elderly Isotta-Fraschini chassis fitted with a new 1400 cc Coventry-Simplex engine. Registered LH 7933, it was completed just in time to compete in the *M.C.C. Brighton Trial* before World War I put a stop to all motor sport, and prevented Lionel Martin from going ahead with his plans to produce a 'sporting light car' which was briefly described in *The Light Car* in November 1914. No further mention was made of the project until November 1919 when *The Motor* published a description of the new Aston Martin car accompanied by an illustration of what appeared to be an identical vehicle to the hybrid but bearing the registration number AM 4656 thus providing us with one of the unsolved mysteries of Aston Martin history for Lionel Martin himself (writing in *Motor Sport* in 1944) related how at the end of the (1st) war a new chassis of A.M. design was assembled, from two supplied by their contractors, with semi-elliptic front suspension and three quarter elliptics at the rear which conforms to a general layout drawing published in the motoring press in 1914 and again in 1919. And yet, Prince Marshall, publisher of that excellent journal *Old Motor*, has recently unearthed a photo of the supposedly post-war car, AM 4656 which clearly shows it had semi-elliptic rear suspension as did the Isotta hybrid which leads one to suspect that AM 4656 was in fact the Isotta LH 7933, re-registered perhaps when the first A.M. engine was fitted, and that the prototype with three quarter elliptic rear suspension was run only briefly, if at all, before being broken up when the design was revised.

However, what is certain is that AM 4656, known at the works as

Coal Scuttle, because of its body shape, ran in the first *J.C.C. 200 Miles Race* and was raced on several later occasions usually driven by Jack Addis.

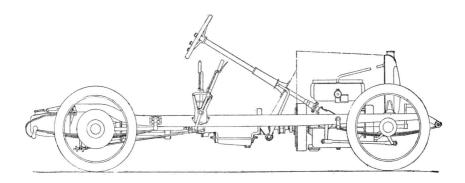

This layout drawing of the proposed Aston Martin light car appeared in the motoring press in 1914.

Jack Addis, the works' foreman, at the wheel of Coal Scuttle.

Taking shape
THE SECOND PROTOTYPE

In 1920 three chassis frames to a revised design with semi-elliptic rear springs had been delivered to the Kensington workshops and in March 1921 *The Autocar* was able to publish a fully illustrated description of what was intended to be the final prototype.

In actual fact only one car was completed to this design for in early trials the frame fractured behind the rear gearbox mounting making further modifications necessary. This first car, with a very ordinary clover leaf body, had a wheelbase of 8' 7½" and was slightly crab tracked, the four foot front track being two inches wider than the rear. The side valve engine followed the general layout of the Coventry-Simplex unit used in *Coal Scuttle* but with helical timing gears in place of chain drive. It had a three bearing crankshaft, drilled connecting rods and Zephyr pistons, also drilled. Particular attention was given to the lubrication system, oil being pressure fed through a series of filters by a spur gear pump situated in the base chamber. The Hele-Shaw multi-plate clutch, fitted with a clutch stop, transmitted the drive through a short open shaft to a separate four speed gearbox mounted stiffly in the frame by four broad webs cast integrally with the gear casing. Final drive was via an enclosed propellor shaft to a fully floating rear axle. Brakes, operating on the rear only, had twin aluminium shoes fitted side by side and operated independently by hand or foot. The steering box, a Marles proprietary unit, was dismantled and carefully re-assembled before fitting, a routine common to all the later production cars and indicative of the extreme care in manufacture demanded by Lionel Martin.

Although the life of this prototype was comparatively brief, the fractured frame was later shortened to form the basis of *Bunny*, a car which was destined to become one of the most famous racing Astons of all time.

Front view of the first prototype chassis. The jacking pads on the front axle are typical of Lionel Martin's attention to detail.

Near side view of the engine of the first prototype. Note the Hele-Shaw clutch and adjustable mounting of the pedal shaft.

Seeds of success
THE FINAL PROTOTYPE

After the prototype frame had revealed a certain weakness in design the tourer was temporarily put to one side together with the two remaining frames of similar specification. Later suitably braced and re-inforced they were converted into the firm's first real racing cars.

Meanwhile in a remarkably short space of time a much stiffer frame was produced in which the side members remained parallel but widened aft of the engine bay. Available in two lengths of wheelbase (8' 9" and 8' 0") the design remained substantially unchanged on all subsequent cars made at Kensington.

In general there was little unusual in the layout but like all Lionel Martin's creations it was beautifully engineered and incorporated many detail refinements which though costly to manufacture, helped put the car in a class of its own. Typical of this attention to detail was the fore and aft adjustment provided for the pedals which were mounted on a common tube pivoting on brackets having serrated bases mating with plates on the chassis frame. Brake and gear levers were splined at their bottom end thus permitting angular adjustment to suit the individual driver.

Oddly enough the coachwork on these earlier Aston Martins often failed to compliment the beautiful chassis, a typical example being a clover leaf tourer in which Lionel Martin himself notched up the car's first race success by winning a short handicap at Brooklands in May 1921 at a speed of 69.75 mph. In the course of its career this particular car was to acquire front wheel brakes and wire wheels as and when these items were introduced on the production models. However, there is reason to suppose that its registration number, AM 270, previously used on the tourer with the broken frame, was later transferred to yet another car altogether. It is an established fact that the works swopped numbers, bodies and engines from car to car as suited the occasion.

With Lionel Martin at the wheel, AM 270 achieved the marque's first race success in the Essex Short Handicap at Brooklands in May 1921.

Lionel Martin at the wheel of AM 270 in one of its early forms.

Achievements extraordinary
THE RACING CAR BUNNY

A.C. Bertelli who in 1926 fathered a new generation of Aston Martins but at this time was racing Enfield-Alldays of his own design, relates how at Brooklands on non-race days Lionel Martin with an entourage consisting of his wife Katherine, H. Kensington-Moir and Jack Addis, would periodically sweep into the paddock with an old Ford van and 'a wretched little car named *Bunny*, which they thought was the be-all-and-end-all of motor cars'. Then, as if by divine right, Martin would have the track cleared of all traffic and send Kensington-Moir out on the little racer to circulate at almost unbelieveable speeds which seemed to increase with each successive visit!

Actually the Kensington equipe had every right to appear confident and perhaps a little arrogant, for *Bunny* really was a most extraordinarily successful racing car with a performance quite out of keeping with its impudent appearance. Built originally with hill climbs in view, it had a very short wheelbase, less than eight feet, and was constructed by cutting and plating one of the first prototype frames. The engine was a standard side valve unit progressively tuned until it was developing 40 bhp at 3800 rpm. Later in its career it sometimes ran with one of the 16 valve *Strasbourg* engines installed and the length of its tail varied from time to time. But it was in side valve form that it achieved eternal fame by becoming the first light car to break world records.

This historic occasion was at *Brooklands* in May 1921 when, starting at 4.30 in the morning, it covered a total of 1275 miles in 16 hours 20 minutes. The drivers were S.C.H. Davis, Clive Gallop and Kensington-Moir. In all they took ten world records.

During a long career, *Bunny* competed in the 1921 *GP des Voiturettes* at Le Mans, in the *J.C.C. 200 Miles Race* in 1921, 1922, 1923 and 1924, the 1922 *Tourist Trophy* in the Isle of Man as well as countless hill climbs and sprint events.

Its ultimate fate is unknown but almost certainly it was broken up many years ago.

Bunny in short tailed form with the well known Bugatti exponent, B.S. Marshall, at the wheel.

The search for power
THE SINGLE OVERHEAD CAMSHAFT ENGINE

Bunny having been successfully built up around the shortened prototype frame, Martin decided to utilise the remaining full length frames, suitably plated and welded, for two special racing cars intended specifically for track racing.

The first of these was completed in the summer of 1921 and weighed some 13½ cwt with side valve engine and rear wheel brakes only. The body built at Kingston by the Hawker aircraft concern, was narrow with high sided cockpit and staggered seats. The second car followed soon afterwards and was almost identical in appearance but was fitted with a new Robb designed 16 valve single overhead camshaft engine of which great things were anticipated. Martin, more than satisfied with the reliability of his little side valve engine, was well aware that it could never match the power output of its more sophisticated rivals boasting overhead valves and he was thus prompted to commission the new engine which was assembled in the toolroom at Rover's. With a bore and stroke of 65 mm x 112 mm (1486 cc), it was of cast iron monobloc construction with a short vertical shaft at the front driving the camshaft which in turn actuated the valves through rockers and push rods. At the front on the offside, the magneto was mounted in a vertical position with water and oil pumps in tandem below, an arrangement which was never completely satisfactory, particularly when appropriated for the later twin cam top half designed by Marcel Gremillon.

Regrettably the general performance of the 16 valve engine was disappointing. It failed to even match the output of *Bunny*'s side valve unit and also suffered from overheating of the valves.

Under pressure from Count Louis Zborowski, who had driven the ohv car in the 200 Miles Race, but with little success, the engine was scrapped and a new twin cam 16 valve layout was designed by Gremillon. Subsequently, the two track cars fitted with side valve and/or twin cam engines, had a long and successful career in the hands of many drivers.

Jack Addis on left, testing the Robb designed 16 valve single overhead camshaft engine. The base chamber incorporating the vertical magento mounting was also utilised for the later twin-cam engine.

One of two similar cars built specifically for use at Brooklands although they were also used for hill climbs. In the picture Count Louis Zborowski is at the wheel with Clive Gallop in the passenger seat. Lionel Martin is directly behind the driver with Jack Addis on his right wearing a cap.

Zborowski's babies

THE STRASBOURG GRAND PRIX CARS

In 1922 the wealthy Count Zborowski, famed for his Brooklands 'monsters', had had some experience with the single cam Aston Martin track cars and was smitten with the urge to compete in the *1500 cc Trophy Race* in the Isle of Man. To this end he financed the construction of two special Astons with 16 valve twin overhead camshaft engines of 65 mm bore x 112 mm stroke. These power units were designed by Marcel Gremillon of the Peugeot company. The French engineer was a protege of Henry, the famous designer of the 3 litre Ballots which inspired his design for the Aston Martin. Unfortunately financial limitations dictated the use of the bottom half of the earlier Robb designed single cam engine which made the new head, cast in one with the block, asymetrical, calling for very large valve pockets which in turn had an unfortunate detrimental effect on their efficiency. They also inherited the vertical magneto drive resulting in their retirement on more than one occasion. Nevertheless they were extremely potent little engines developing 55 bhp at 4200 rpm. The chassis with wire wheels and front wheel brakes were very similar to the final design adopted for the standard s.v. cars which were to shortly to enter production.

As events turned out the two cars were not ready for the Isle of Man race and were entered for the *French Grand Prix* held at Strasbourg later in the year. This race was run to a 2 litre formula with a minimum weight limit of 750 kg, so the Aston Martins of only 1486 cc capacity, gave away half a litre to their competitors as well as having some inbuilt weight in order to comply with the regulations.

At Strasbourg Zborowski was partnered by his great confrere Clive Gallop and both cars ran splendidly until retiring with problems attributed to the magneto drive. Then followed the *GP de Penya Rhin* at Barcelona where the Count came second behind Divo on one of the invincible Talbots.

Some half dozen additional twin cam engines were built and raced in a variety of Astons including the veteran *Bunny*. They also found their way into racing boats.

Off side view of the twin cam 16 valve engine. The layout of the Robb design-ed bottom half inherited from his aborted single cam engine is clearly seen.

Clive Gallop at Strasbourg with one of the original pair of Grand Prix cars.

Take any number

THE STRANGE STORY OF THE STRASBOURG CARS

As we have seen, Lionel Martin had a strange habit of swopping number plates from car to car, a procedure that for many years obscured the later history of the 1922/23 *Strasbourg* racers.

Now, Fred Ellis, the noted authority on B & M Astons, has recently established that there were in fact three sixteen valve works' cars and not two as had been generally supposed. In the light of this new information it is possible to clarify the rather complicated story of the three cars and their subsequent history. After the 1922 French Grand Prix the car driven by Zborowski was purchased by R.C. Morgan who specified a side valve engine and full road equipment. For some inexplicable reason, Lionel Martin gave it the number plates (XL 3125) off Gallop's car which was purchased by G.E.T. Eyston complete with 16 valve engine and bearing the number XL 2445 off Zborowski's car. With the sobriquet 'Green Pea' inscribed on the bonnet, R.C. Morgan, together with Mrs Agnew, raced their side valve engined racer most successfully and at a later date fitted a Hooker-Thomas engine and in May 1925 it was re-registered as a Thomas Special with the number PE 2516, which it bears to this day having been restored with an A.M. s.v. engine by Neil Murray.

Meanwhile Eyston's ex-Gallop car was taken back by the works, fitted with a side valve engine and sold to R.G. Barlow under yet another registration number, ORI. It then became the property of Major Frank Halford who in turn fitted a rather splendid six cylinder engine of his own design, calling the car a Halford Special. Fred Ellis recently purchased the remains of the chassis and has restored it using an A.M. 16 valve engine. At the same time he has been able to re-register it as XL 2445, which number it had when owned by Eyston.

And the third car? This was assembled by the works after the original pair of Grand Prix cars had been disposed of to Morgan and Eyston. Registered XP 3037 it was raced in 1923 by Zborowski in the G.P. de Penya Rhin at Barcelona and by Gallop at the Spanish Sitges track. The subject of yet another splendid Ellis restoration, it now reposes in the National Motor Museum at Beaulieu.

Clive Gallop and Zborowski before the start of the French Grand Prix at Strasbourg in 1922.

Green Pea, the 1922 ex-works car raced with side valve engine by R.C. Morgan, whose declaration 'Coachwork by Strachan and Brown of Kensington High Street' on his entry form for the 1923 Grand Prix de Boulogne did not compare with the names of the exotic carosserie registered by his Continental rivals and caused him some embarrassment.

Brilliant failure

THE SINGLE SEATER RAZOR BLADE

Razor Blade with a maximum width of only 18½" was conceived with but one object in view, to be the first light car to exceed 100 mph. Martin knew that A.C. had such a record in mind and was determined to scotch their plans but he was unsuccessful. *Razor Blade* was a brute to handle and had a nasty habit of throwing its offside front tyre when coming off the banking at the Brooklands' fork.

Although quite the most special and unorthodox Aston Martin of all time it is remarkable how stock components were cleverly adapted and utilised in its construction.

The frame narrowed sharply behind the 16 valve twin cam engine to barely eighteen inches and remained parallel to the rear where two large brackets supported the quarter elliptic springs. These springs were so stiff, that they were almost inflexible and in the opinion of Fred Ellis, who owned the car some years ago, were largely the reason for the car's bad handling characteristics.

The rear axle with a track of only three feet was built up around a standard diff casing with 6" inboard brakes providing metal to metal contact which were almost completely useless. The brakeless front axle with four foot track was fared off with wooden formers. Sankey wheels were used all round but later changed to wire pattern.

The body, built by the de Haviland aircraft concern, had a hinged cockpit cover almost totally enclosing the driver, but after preliminary tests, several changes were made including the abandonment of the closed cockpit.

Although it failed to achieve its objective, *Razor Blade* did eventually turn out to be quite a successful racer with a maximum speed of around 110 mph in the hands of Capt. J.C. Douglas and Major Frank Halford who became a famous designer of aircraft engines, notably the Napier 'Sabre' and the Napier-Halford 'Dagger'.

Razor Blade was the most specialised of all Lionel Martin's creations and was cleverly conceived but never quite lived up to expectations. It is seen here in an early form before the fitting of wire wheels.

This picture of Razor Blade's chassis taken during Fred Ellis' painstaking restoration in 1967, reveals the almost solid rear suspension, narrow track and inboard brakes.

Escape through the back door
THE PRE-PRODUCTION CARS

Although the Aston Martin appeared in *The Autocar* 'Buyer's Guide', as early as 1920, virtually no cars had been sold some three years later. Lionel Martin, encouraged by his wife and his protege H. Kensington-Moir, seemed pre-occupied with racing which no doubt they were able to excuse on the grounds of development.

With half a dozen cars (the two GP cars, the pair of track racers, *Bunny* and AM 270) all active in competition almost every week-end it is small wonder they did not get down to serious product-ion. With a staff of only twenty or so it must have taxed all their resources to build and service the racers and the cost must have been formidable.

However, by 1923 when serious production plans were beginning to take priority one or two cars had somehow been put together from surplus parts and these had passed into private hands. Most noticeable of these was a side valve two seater with Sankey wheels and rear wheel brakes which was in many respects a near replica of *Bunny*. Painted black with aluminium bonnet it was named *Nigger* and was the first car sold to a private owner. Its purchaser was Capt. J.C. Douglas who raced it quite a bit before acquiring *Razor Blade* which he bravely managed to tame where others had failed.

Her racing days over, *Nigger* was equipped as a road car for R.W. Mallabar. With quickly detachable wings painted red, with the body in grey, it is hoped that she had lost her offensive name.

A second early pre-production model was a heavy looking four seater all-weather tourer on the long chassis also with Sankey wheels and rear wheel brakes. Nothing is known of this vehicle except that its photograph graced the pages of Bamford and Martin's catalogue as late as 1925.

Bearing the unfortunate name Nigger, this long chassis two seater raced by the works was later purchased by R.W. Mallabar who fitted full road equipment.

This early 'all weather tourer' was still pictured in the manufacturers' catalogue long after the marque had acquired wire wheels and front wheel brakes.

Deliveries have commenced

THE PRODUCTION ASTON MARTIN

In February 1922 H. Kensington-Moir took *Bunny* up the Brooklands test hill in a record time of 9.29 seconds, an achievement that prompted Bamford and Martin to take a full page advertisement in *The Light Car and Cyclecar*, and thereafter through the whole of 1922 they advertised their racing and record accomplishments in the motor journals of the time, *The Autocar*, *The Motor, The Auto* and *The Light Car*. But it was not until early the following year that their publicity proclaimed that 'Deliveries have commenced and cars are being booked for delivery in strict rotation'.

Prices quoted were £695 for the sports 2 and 3 seaters and £720 for the full four seater on the long chassis. These prices however could only have served as a guide to the prospective owner, for Bamford and Martin had no coachbuilding facilities and almost every body produced was an individual design by one of the smaller specialist coachbuilders, Jarvis of Wimbledon, Comptons of Hersham and Albany of Hanwell. Moss of Fulham Road were responsible for several almost identical fabric bodied clover leaf models which were as near to being a 'standard' Aston model as any produced.

In spite of its racing pedigree, a very large number of long wheel base chassis were fitted with touring bodies. There were even two or three saloons but these seem to have been replaced with open coachwork quite early in their life. Indeed, the swopping of coachwork was not at all unusual in the twenties and quite a few Astons had replacement bodies fitted by the original or subsequent owners.

The first true production car with wire wheels and front wheel brakes was chassis number 1919 (numbers started at 1900) supplied to a Mr Greenall and the last car of which there is any record, was no. 1969, an Albany bodied model exhibited at Olympia in 1925. The last car to be sold however was no. 1967 being one of the assets taken over by the new company after B & M went into liquidation. It was delivered in 1926 from the Feltham works where servicing of the original cars was carried on for a number of years.

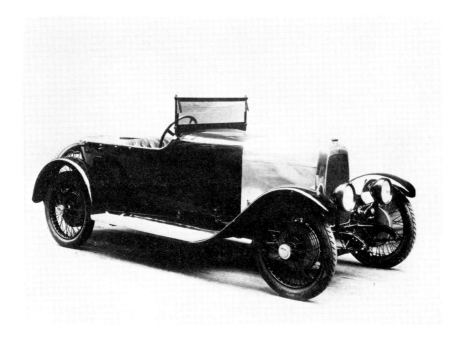

Built to individual order no two Bamford and Martin Astons were identical, but if any model could be described as typical of the marque, then this lovely clover-leaf sports tourer warrants that description. But so varied were the individual body styles, it would be virtually impossible to collect pictures of every type, so a representative selection is featured in the following pages.

This racy two seater had its body finished in machine turned aluminium, an expensive fad popular during the twenties.

Another sporting two seater with coachwork by W.W. Hall of Redditch.

Early prototype and racing Astons had brakes on the rear wheels only, but following the building of the Strasbourg cars, all production models had front brakes operated on the Perrot system.

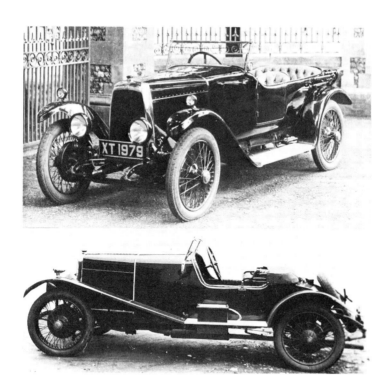

Suggesting a small 30/98 Vauxhall, this splendid long chassis tourer was delivered to the Rev. Capt. Ward in 1924, but he later discarded the full four seater body in favour of a distinctly sporting two seater.

A standard side valve engine dismantled during restoration by P.N. Delves-Broughton.

Despite the phenomenal success of Lionel Martin's cars in competition, he managed to secure only one order for the full blooded Grand Prix replica listed at £725 in chassis form and this to a Swiss client.

Lionel Martin seated on the chassis of the 'Swiss' car before despatch to the coachbuilders Messrs Strachan and Brown who after building aircraft during World War I went on to produce buses and coaches of superb quality.

Not all Astons were sports cars as this stylish saloon and practical tourer illustrates.

Although closed models were distinctly rare this example by an unknown coachbuilder shows just how splendid they could be.

Astons in the antipodes
THREE SIDE VALVERS IN AUSTRALIA

Australia between the two world wars could boast of a very know-
ledgeable and enthusiastic hard core of motorists who between
them were responsible for importing at least one of almost every
make of car in the world but it is nevertheless remarkable that no
less than three side valve Aston Martins found their way out there.

Alf Fairfax, whose family published Sydney's leading daily paper,
whilst on a visit to England, purchased two almost identical
fabric bodied clover leaf models, distinguishable only by the
mounting of the side lamps on the front wings of one of the pair.
Back home, Fairfax raced both cars with a fair measure of success
until disposing of them in 1930. Since then one has completely
disappeared and the second, known as the *Wangaratta* car after
the small town in Victoria, where it was run to earth by the
writer's wife in 1946, was vandalised when the original engine was
replaced by a bronze head 12/50 Alvis unit. The third 'Australian
Aston' was a short chassis side valve car with the small radiator,
Strasbourg style body and flowing wings reminiscent of the
Salmsons of the period. This interesting car was built in 1924 to
the order of a Major Harold Hall of London, who passed it on
to a relative, Mr John E. Goodall of Melbourne.

Goodall competed throughout Victoria in all manner of events
and in 1927 he had it fitted with a new two seater body by
Messrs G.P. Motors of 57 City Road, South Melbourne. He raced
it in this form in the first Australian Grand Prix held on the
Philip Island circuit in 1928 and again in 1930 when it came
7th after every other green car had crashed or retired.

Imported to Australia in 1924, this side valve two seater with the rare G.P. radiator remained in the same family for more than fifty years. Early in its life it was fitted with a new body of local manufacture.

Another 'Australian' side valve car was this fabric bodied clover leaf, one of a pair imported to New South Wales by Alf Fairfax. After the war it became the property of the author's wife but a subsequent owner sadly vandalised it.

The success that might have been
THE BENSON TWIN-CAM ENGINE

The Hon. John Benson was a great enthusiast whose knowledge of motor car design was distinctly academic and so when he assumed his directorship of Bamford and Martin Ltd he quickly enlisted the vast practical experience of Lionel Martin and Jack Addis in designing a new engine intended to bring the Aston Martin right up to date and consolidate the firm's future. But fate was to decree otherwise. A run of bad luck and sheer misfortune delayed development of the new power unit and they had inadequate finance with which to weather the storm beyond an expensive showing at Olympia in 1925.

The new engine was a twin overhead camshaft affair with 8 valves in a detachable head mated up to a machined Strasbourg block which led to the perpetuation of the old measurements of 65 mm x 112 mm bore and stroke. At the same time the old Robb designed bottom half was also retained. In Charnwood's own words 'It was initially something of a bodge-up'. Even so it showed great potential, developing 60 bhp at 4200 rpm on the test bench and was expected to do well in the 1924 *200 Miles Race* for which a special streamlined car had been built. Misfortune number one occurred when the car crashed on its journey from the coachbuilders and could not be repaired in time.

It was then loaned to Major Johnson-Noad for trial in a new speed boat he was having built for the Duke of York's Trophy which he had won the previous year using one of the Strasbourg engines. Foolishly the designer of the hull thought that B & M were exaggerating in claiming a 15% increase in power over the earlier 16 valve units and on its first trials 'Pampiro' turned on her propellor axis and Benson's pride and glory went to the bottom. On being salvaged it was restarted still filled with Thames mud and that was the end of that!

However, the new engine had proved itself a worthwhile proposition and Benson received the go-ahead to design a new block and bottom half with a revised bore and stroke of 73 mm x 89 mm, in which form it showed 64 bhp at 4500 rpm on the test bench, where its spur camshaft gears rang out so loud and clear, that it was named *Caruso*. Once again hopes were centred on the *200 Miles Race* (of 1925) but the engine could not be readied in time. Suitably buffed and polished it was the centrepiece of the firm's display at Olympia. Alas it was too late. The end had come for Bamford and Martin who did not survive to develop the engine which had showed such promise. Retained by its designer it proved extremely reliable being driven for 125,000 miles without so much as having the big ends taken up and this even after being super-charged with a Zoller blower as Benson had originally intended.

A later owner dismantled the car, engine and chassis became separated, their ultimate fate uncertain.

Bamford and Martin's swan song was the twin overhead camshaft 8 valve engine designed by the Hon. John Benson.

Bad luck twice over

BAMFORD & MARTIN'S LAST TWO RACERS

When the Charnwoods assumed control of Bamford and Martin, the small work force was channeled into assembling production cars. All the works' racers had been sold off to private owners, although no doubt some of these were still being serviced by the manufacturers. However, neither Lionel Martin nor the Hon. John Benson were at all anxious to abstain completely from competition and between them they planned one new racer for the 1924 *200 Miles Race* to be powered by the new twin cam 8 valve engine.

The new car was built up around a standard long chassis with a particularly well streamlined aluminium body. This had a high sided cockpit, full length under shield and almost completely enclosed radiator with a small aperture in the cowling. Great things were expected of this car but by a cruel stroke of luck it was badly damaged whilst being towed from the coachbuilders. Lionel Martin, in the towing vehicle, indulged in a mild race with another car, forgetting or not appreciating that the racer, not yet fitted with its engine was light at the front end and that John Benson was having difficulty in controlling it. As this happened only a few days before the race, it was obviously a non-starter.

The following year another new car was built for the *200 Miles Race* with a *Strasbourg* engine, the Benson engine with new bottom half not being ready in time. Not as fully streamlined as the previous year's car it had a fabric body by Gordon England. In fitting an apron over the front dumb irons, the first cross member was eliminated and the shock absorbers mounted inside the frame, which made the car unsteady and Humphrey Cook crashed on the first lap of the race. Hitting the rails after the fork, the car overturned injuring the mechanic; Cook escaped with bruises. John Benson, in later years, attributed the cause of the accident directly to the changes made to the front end.

And so on this sad note the racing activities of Bamford and Martin came to a close, although cars bearing the little round radiator badge appeared in private hands for some years to follow and thirty or forty years later *Razor Blade, Green Pea* and *Strasbourg* cars and others, all beautifully restored, came back to life as worthy participants of the post-war vintage scene.

Intended to be powered by the original Benson twin cam engine, this stream-lined racer was built for the 1924 J.C.C. 200 miles race but was wrecked en route from the coachbuilders and never rebuilt.

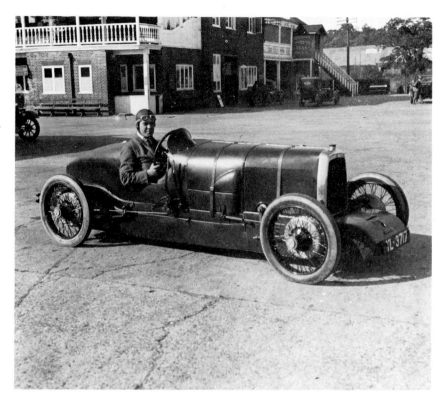

The following year a new car was prepared for the 200 miles, using the second Benson twin cam engine. Driven by H.W. Cook it crashed on the first lap, a sad finish to the competition history of the Kensington firm.

PART II

1926 - 1935

A.C. BERTELLI'S 1.5 LITRES

A.C. Bertelli, designer, engineer and racing driver. Directly responsible for all
Aston Martins built at Feltham between 1927 and 1936; his was a constant
battle against financial adversity.

INTRODUCTION

'It is indeed rare that one finds a designer with sufficient grasp of his subject to be able to follow the construction of his car from the drawing board, through all stages of experiment and manufacture, until he finally drives it to success in an important event; and when one finds such a man his products are bound to be something to reckon with in competitions'.

Thus did *Motor Sport* describe the man who was to play the leading role in the renaissance of the Aston Martin car and for a period of ten years contributed so much skill and practical experience to the design and development of what was to become one of the finest sports cars this country has ever produced.

Augustus Cesare Bertelli, known as 'Bert' to his colleagues and 'Gus' to his family and closest friends, was an Italian by birth, but an Englishman or more correctly a Welshman by force of circumstances. His father, disliking the political climate in Italy, had immigrated with his family to Cardiff in 1894, where Bertelli together with his elder brother Enrico (known as 'Harry') was brought up and educated.

As a lad, A.C. Bertelli was very fond of football and boxing and after leaving school at the age of fourteen, played Rugby for Cardiff. Had this not been so, the British motor industry might well have been denied one of its most brilliant engineers, because, motivated by curiosity, Bertelli returned to the land of his birth only to discover that football, indeed all games, were prohibited on Sundays. He returned to Britain after only a twelve months stay during which time (he was then 18/19 years of age), he worked in the Fiat experimental department under the supervision of the great Felice Nazarro with whom he rode as mechanic in the *Targo Bologna*, which they won. Thus a love of speed was added to his love of football. In Britain he reckoned he could have both!

At the outbreak of the first world war he was working on aero engines for the Grahame-White Aviation company at Hendon and it was here that he met his future wife Vera. Whilst at Hendon as a personal exercise, he designed a rotary internal combustion engine similar in principle to the modern Wankel unit but was prevented from actually building one as its creation infringed his terms of employment with Grahame-White and after a bit of a showdown with his employers he left having been invited by the Birmingham firm of Enfield and Allday to test and appraise an advanced radial engined car which they planned to put into early production in order to catch the anticipated post-war boom for new cars.

It was immediately evident to Bertelli that the prototype car would require lengthy and costly development and, always blunt and honest, he told its sponsors so in no uncertain terms. They were doubtless taken aback by his criticism but not only did they accept his professional opinion, they offered him the position of designer and general manager with instructions to produce a more acceptable vehicle in time for the London motor show of the following year, 1921.

Skilfully salvaging as many parts from the original radial engined car as possible (hundreds of transmission gears were already in stock) and by building a new conventional 4 cylinder engine of 1488 cc, Bertelli met his directive and the new 10 hp Enfield-Allday with bodies by his brother Harry Bertelli was ready as promised. Not only were pre-production models on display at Olympia, but in the same month Bertelli was racing one of the new cars at Brooklands in the *J.C.C. 200 Miles Race*. He finished 16th overall. Quite a promising beginning.

The 1922 Enfield-Allday sports model designed by A.C. Bertelli with coachwork by his brother Enrico before they were jointly concerned with the rejuvenation of the Aston Martin.

From the Bertelli family album comes this rare picture of Buzz Box, the one and only R & B car which directly preceeded the 'new' Aston Martin. Based on an Enfield-Allday chassis it was powered by a single overhead camshaft engine designed by Bertelli in collaboration with his partner, W.S. Renwick.

The R & B engine as developed for production in the 'new' Aston Martin. The fan was soon found unnecessary and discarded as was the costly scuttle mounted steering box.

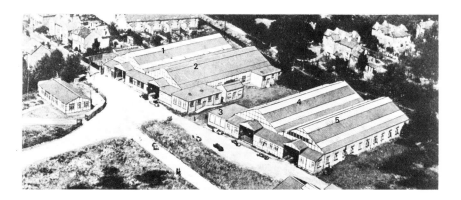

The works at Feltham where so much Aston Martin history was made. 1) The 'end shop' occupied by E. Bertelli Ltd when the coachbuilding side of the business became an independent concern in 1930. 2) This shop, not held on a permanent lease, was vacant most of the time being used as service department only when trade was booming during the later thirties. 3) The engine test house equipped with two Heenan and Froude dynamometers and ruled over by the late Joe Bestante, a master engine tuner. 4) This shop was shared between the well equipped machine tool department and assembly of engines, gearboxes and axles. 5) The chassis assembly shop shared in slack periods with the service department.

Early days at Feltham with the first T-type tourer nearing completion. Immediately behind can be glimpsed the R & B Buzz Box with a second tourer body in course of construction alongside. The gentleman on the left with cigarette, is the seldom photographed Harry (Enrico) Bertelli, who designed and built all the production bodies on his brother's 1½ litre chassis.

The following year with sales of standard models more than fulfilling expectations he was able to build three special racers which he ran in the Isle of Man *Tourist Trophy Race* and again in the *200 Miles Race* as well as many lesser events. Already he was exercising a policy of development through racing; a routine he learned from his year with Fiats and was to follow throughout his career as a motor engineer.

But, as he seemed fated to experience so many times throughout his career, success was punctuated by a major set back. Messrs Alldays and Onions, the parent company of Enfield-Allday, lost money on other projects and in the ensueing liquidation the motor car subsidiary was dragged down with them, leaving Bertelli out of a job. Never at his happiest working for a faceless management he turned down several offers and set up on his own as a freelance consultant doing work for Armstrong-Siddeley, Coventry-Simplex, Rover and other companies.

Then around this time 'Wolf' Barnato, who had driven in the Enfield-Allday team (and was later to achieve fame as financier and driver of Bentleys), decided he would like to become a motor manufacturer and as a first step employed Bertelli to design a new motor car. Three prototypes were built by the designer himself at the Barnato mansion at Lingfield in Surrey. The engines utilised single sleeve valves and in order to put these to a preliminary test, were mounted in three ex-racing Enfield-Allday chassis and entered as 'Bertelli' cars for the 1923 *200 Miles Race.* Although fast in practise they proved troublesome in the actual race and obviously required further development. This probably did not unduly worry their millionaire sponsor but the election of the first Labour Government most certainly did and he scuttled off to the USA, firmly believeing he was to be relieved of his fortune.

Once again the unfortunate Bertelli was left high and dry, and sadly, with the abandonment of this latest project he had foregone the right to use his own name on any car he might build in the future. However, good fortune then brought William Somerville

Renwick into the story. Renwick was a talented young designer who had met Bertelli at Armstrong-Siddeleys and having just inherited a substantial fortune, invited the out of work engineer to join him in 'making a motor car'. A tempting offer indeed, but Bertelli considered the money insufficient to cover the design and development of a complete vehicle so he suggested they build a proprietary engine, which if efficient and competitive might well sell in quantities of several hundred a year. This was the heyday of the assembled motor car with dozens of smaller manufacturers buying their engines, gearboxes and axles from outside specialists. So, confident they could compete in the engine field, the firm of Renwick and Bertelli Ltd was set up in a small machine shop in the Kings Road at Tysely, a suburb of Birmingham. One of their first employees was a young trainee draughtsman named Claude Hill who came to them direct from school and was to remain with Bertelli for ten years and go on to play a prominent role in the Aston Martin story. The immediate outcome of the new partnership was a tough four cylinder 1500 cc engine with a single overhead camshaft operating valves situated in such a manner that they provided the much desired turbulent effect with a compact combustion chamber typical of overhead valve engines. This arrangement was the subject of British patent no 247729 dated February 25th 1926.

For a mobile test bed Bertelli once more fell back on one of his old Enfield-Allday chassis which after being fitted with the new engine was registered as the 'R & B' but was better known to the small staff as 'Buzzbox'.

Between them the two partners covered many thousands of miles in this special and just when they decided the engine was ready for volume production they received a proposition from the Hon John Benson whose family had recently purchased the assets and goodwill of the ailing Bamford and Martin company for £10,000 and having done so did not quite know how to proceed from there. Renwick and Bertelli were invited to visit the old B & M premises in Kensington with a view to forming some sort of amalgamation. The two men were astonished at what they

The Mark II assembly line in 1935. To the right is the service area and at the far end the new car delivery bay.

The machine shop with Mark II cylinder castings awaiting machining and partly assembled engines on the right.

Coachbuilding as a fine art. Mark II bodies, 2/4 seaters, saloons and (far right) one of the rare drophead coupes.

saw. In Bertelli's own words 'little more than a mews garage with a lathe, a small milling machine and power drill'.

Lionel Martin had gone through a small fortune leaving nothing more tangible than a name ... ASTON MARTIN. But that was sufficient for Bertelli who was quick to appreciate the commercial value of such a name, if their own unknown company of Renwick and Bertelli were eventually to produce a complete new car incorporating their R & B power unit.

On the 12th of October 1926 the firm of Aston Martin Motors Ltd was duly incorporated, the directors being the Charnwoods, father and son, and Renwick and Bertelli. A 'real' factory was leased at Feltham where the war time works of the Whitehead Aircraft concern was being divided into industrial blocks. Comprehensive machine tools were installed together with the necessary facilities for coachwork production, a department which was organised and managed by Harry Bertelli. Later this was to become a separate company, E. Bertelli Ltd, with A.C. Bertelli's wife Vera as Chairman and Treasurer, because her husband was barred from holding office in any business other than Aston Martin.

From the very beginning John Benson and Renwick, both theoretical rather than practical engineers, were at loggerheads in the work they shared in the drawing office and Bertelli had to act as referee on several occasions making sure that the final designs were in accordance with his own overall conception.

The new Aston Martin made its debut at Olympia in 1927, not the most favourable time in which to introduce what was by its very nature a rich man's plaything. The slump was gaining momentum and the cost of setting up the factory together with development had devoured much of the company's capital and they were in financial trouble almost from the beginning. Benson was the first to throw in his hand followed soon afterwards by Renwick, his inheritance sadly depleted. Bertelli with little or no personal wealth, stubbornly hung on and the company was reformed as Aston Martin Ltd with fresh finance coming from S.C. Whitehouse, a Harrow garage proprietor who had wealthy connections, Nigel Holder and Straker of Messrs Kensington-Moir and Straker who were the car's distributors. Additional finance was provided by P.C. 'Percy' Kidner, an old friend of Bertelli's who for many years had been joint managing director of Vauxhalls up to the time they were taken over by the American General Motors. Having nurtured the famous 30/98 Vauxhall, Kidner obviously knew a good motor car when he saw one and was terrifically enthusiastic over the Aston Martin.

However enthusiastic as was every member of this group, their joint investment was insufficient to maintain the firm for very long, particularly as Bertelli continued his costly racing programme as a means of development. By 1931 the firm was in real trouble once more. Bertelli on his own admittance had been too ambitious (costwise) in tackling a completely individual design and he was compelled to more or less pawn the company to the late H.J. Aldington of Frazer-Nash cars, who took over responsibility for sales. With the Frazer-Nash selling at exactly half the price of the Aston Martin, such an arrangement could not hope to have been permanent and although Aldington was generous and sympathetic, Bertelli by nature was unhappy at having lost his independence. His saviour was a London motor dealer named Lance Prideaux-Brune who invested sufficient capital for the firm to regain its independence and to enable Bertelli to revise his design in such a manner that production costs could be considerably reduced which he did by utilising proprietary gearboxes and rear axles.

This was a wise and successful change of heart for the new car won the *Rudge Whitworth Cup* at Le Mans in 1932 which lead to the introduction of the *Le Mans* model which sold in greater numbers than any previous A.M. But even so the company was still not showing a profit and Prideaux-Brune could no longer support the manufacturing side of the business, although he retained the distribution concession at his modern Winter Garden garage in Holborn.

Then almost from 'out of the blue' came Sir Arthur Sutherland who had considerable shipping interests centred in Newcastle. He virtually bought out the company and installed his son, R. Gordon Sutherland, as joint managing director with Bertelli, the plan being that Bertelli should continue as Technical Director with Gordon Sutherland responsible for sales and service. Sutherland had spent some time in the drawing office at Alvis after receiving a Diploma with Honours at The Automobile Engineering College at Chelsea, and therefore had some knowledge of engineering, although lacking the practical experience of Bertelli. Unfortunately the two men did not always agree on policy and their relationship was not as smooth as might have been desirable. In particular Bertelli was convinced of the value of racing to a company like Aston Martin, whereas Sir Arthur Sutherland was not as enthusiastic considering it an expensive luxury that interfered with production.

However, both men in their different ways, were equally determined to see the marque prosper and achieve even greater acclaim. Between them they set up the *Le Mans* model on a proper production basis and it was a most successful car succeeded in 1934 by the Mark II version. At Le Mans in 1935 the *Rudge Cup* (or Bi-ennial Cup as it had been renamed) was won yet again and the marque put up the fastest lap in its class three years in succession. At Ulster they won the team award in both 1934 and 1935.

A production version of the work's team cars was then made available to wealthy amateurs in whose hands it gained many successes throughout Europe. Known as the *Ulster*, it was one of the last great sports cars of the vintage era and has been described as legendary, although the number still in existence gives it much greater substance.

Sadly, behind the scenes the gulf between Bertelli and Sutherland was increasing. Perhaps each found it difficult to bridge a generation gap of twenty years? Whatever the reason, in 1937 Bertelli who was developing a new 2 litre model, resigned from the company. He never again built a motor car and eventually at the age of sixty, started a new and equally brilliant career as agriculturist and champion pig breeder. Today he lives in retirement more proud perhaps of his Smithfield trophies than he is of the handsome Rudge-Whitworth Cup which adorns his lounge, although when he is shown one of 'his' Astons he glows with pride and talks of 'the good old days'.

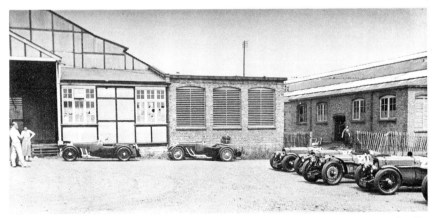

Racers and team tenders assembled in the works yard before departure for Le Mans in 1934.

The works convoy en route for Le Mans. The racers head the column with Miss Bean's 2/4 seater taking up the rear behind the factory 'truck' piled high with the equipe's baggage.

First of a new breed

THE T-TYPE SALOON AND TOURER

Advertised as 'The car that is built for the owner's pleasure', the new Aston Martin, available as a four seater tourer and coachbuilt saloon, made its first appearance at the 1927 Olympia Show.

The chassis was of basically conventional layout for the period, upswept over both axles and hung on semi-elliptic springs but in detail it displayed much original thought on the part of the designer. Massive steel lined aluminium brake drums of 14" diameter were a distinctive feature as was the mounting of the steering box high on the aluminium framed bulkhead providing a near vertical steering wheel position. This proved expensive to assemble accurately and was soon abandoned in favour of a conventional Marles steering box mounted on the frame. The worm drive rear axle with aluminium sleeves was unusual but despite progressive modifications was a fragile component and was never completely satisfactory. Bertelli himself wistfully confesses 'I never did make a decent rear axle!' But he did make a magnificent little gearbox of which he is still immensely proud. This was a four speed box with straight cut gears and right-hand lever. It proved to be very tough and reliable and, with centre change, was used on all the later sports models right through to the last Mark IIs in 1935. The engine of course was a four cylinder overhead camshaft unit which had been thoroughly tested in the one-off Renwick and Bertelli car.

The bodies, designed and built by Bertelli's brother Harry, were extremely handsome. The tourer with long flowing wings was of sporting appearance yet eminently practical, seating four persons in considerable comfort although its rather excessive weight curtailed performance, top speed being only 70 mph. Listed at £550 it was considerably cheaper than the earlier B & M cars, but still expensive as was the saloon at £675 and only eight examples were sold during the two years it was in production.

The saloon was particularly attractive in appearance, with a V-fronted screen and fabric covered roof and rear quarters. Only nine examples were built.

The handsome T-type saloon of 1928. Earlier examples had the chassis frame exposed between the bottom of the doors and the running boards.

The Hon John Benson standing beside the first T-type tourer accentuates the car's low build.

73

The shape of things to come
THE 1927 THREE SEATER SPORTS

Also exhibited at Olympia in 1927 was a pretty little sports model with a three seater clover leaf body. Although catalogued at £575 it was in fact only a hurriedly prepared mock-up by no means ready for production. According to the late Lord Charnwood (formerly the Hon. John Benson) it would never have run anyway! But it was indicative of the direction in which Bertelli's new car was to develop in the future.

By utilising a stock Rubery Owen frame, cut and welded so that the rear end passed under the axle, a very low chassis line was achieved which foreshadowed the famous *International* models. The major mechanical components, engine, gearbox and axles were the same as used in the *T* types with the power unit suitably modified with higher compression, twin carburettors and dual ignition. The latter feature was apparently experimental and not persisted with. Wet sump lubrication was retained with plunger oil pump later to be superseded by gear type. The close fitting cycle pattern wings bolted to the brake torque plates and the 21" wheels were to become a distinctive feature of Aston Martin sports models right up to the introduction of the 2 litre models in 1936.

A minor point of interest on this prototype was the first use of the winged radiator badge, the early *T* types having the original small A.M. monogram inherited from the side valve cars built at Kensington.

The hastily prepared sports 'mock-up' exhibited at Olympia in 1927. Built up around a shortened proprietary frame it clearly suggested the shape of things to come.

The twin carburettor sports engine fitted to the car illustrated above. The twin ignition was purely experimental and not continued with.

Racing once more

THE 1928 WORKS' CARS

Bertelli had always believed racing to be the quickest and most efficient method of strenuous development and was soon busy organising a team for the 1928 *24 Hours Race* at Le Mans.

Two cars were built on 8' 6" wheelbase underslung chassis designed in the works and not fabricated assemblies as used on the prototype sports exhibited at Olympia. The regulation three seater bodies were of attractive design but spoilt by ugly 'banana' type wings secured by blacksmith's stays at the rear and mounted on modified T type lamp pillars and cross bar at the front, which together with the offside spare wheel resulted in a generally untidy appearance.

A major technical innovation, rare in the automobile world, was the adoption of dry sump lubrication, a 2 gallon oil reservoir being mounted between the front dumb irons and concealed by a neat louvred apron. Carburettors were twin SU and for the first time a central gear lever was used. This was extremely short for the period (6") and operated through a little gate with a hinged reverse catch. A conventional Marles steering box replaced the scuttle mounted unit of the standard cars and was to become standard practise on subsequent production cars.

As was the custom in those days the two cars were driven to Le Mans and during the high speed run across France a serious weakness revealed itself in the rear axle sleeves, one of them collapsing completely. On arrival at the circuit they were repaired and strengthened with tie rods at the Morris-Leon Bollee factory.

So even before starting in the race a valuable lesson had been learned.

Although both cars eventually retired the marque was awarded the special Rudge-Whitworth prize of 1000 francs for the fastest lap by a 1½ litre car in the first twenty laps and in so doing, established a long association with that event.

The first works racers to be built at Feltham used a new chassis frame, underslung at the rear and dry sump lubrication.

The use of T-type wing supports and the high mounting of the head lamps tended to detract from the racer's otherwise splendid frontal appearance.

Racer into demonstrator
LM 1 RE-VAMPED

Following the 1928 Le Mans race one of the team cars was tidied up and transformed into the prototype of the new catalogued sports model, forerunner of the famous *International* 2/4 seater which was to become the mainstay of Aston Martin production for the next three years.

This particular car, chassis number LM I (all Bertelli's racing Astons bore the prefix LM) was road tested by *The Autocar* in February 1929 and described as being 'too good a machine to be produced in ones and twos', but with the general slump enveloping the country, it is remarkable that Aston Martins were able to survive at all, let alone increase production beyond this figure.

After serving a term as work's demonstrator, LM 1 passed into the hands of S.C.H. 'Sammy' Davis, a close personal friend of Bertelli. Today Sammy refers to it as 'my beloved Aston'. During his long period of ownership, during which time he never once put up the hood, the car was rebodied with external fuel tank at the rear and in 1932 proudly bore the new enamel radiator badge designed by Sammy Davis himself but his was unique in that it was black whereas the style adopted by the works was cream.

The car still exists today in the hands of a Canadian enthusiast.

After Le Mans the original team car (No. LM I), generally tidied up and fitted with cycle wings, which were to become traditional Aston Martin feature, was used as work's demonstrator.

With smaller radiator than those used on later production cars and three seater body conforming to Le Mans regulations, the ex-team car was very shapely when viewed from above.

Wet or dry sump?
VARIATIONS AT OLYMPIA 1928

Following the successful use of the dry sump engine at Le Mans, Aston Martin tentatively offered a sports model with a similar power unit and this was exhibited at Olympia alongside a second sports model with the original wet sump engine as used in the long chassis touring cars which were still available, probably from stock.

The dry sump car was fitted with the cycle wings first shown the previous year whereas the more conventional sports model had long sweeping wings and broad running boards. Of the two models exhibited it was the dry sump version that claimed the attention of the enthusiasts and was to become a feature of the marque for the next ten years.

Like so many small motor manufacturers at that time, Aston Martin had to feel their way into an uncertain specialist market before deciding exactly what type of car they were going to offer. They could not afford to spread their resources over too wide a range. Up to this time they had been a little indecisive but acceptance of the dry sump engine indicated the path they should follow and during the following twelve months they rationalised their programme around this unit.

After the Show the wet sump sports car (No S4) was retained as work's guinea pig and eventually after being fitted with a dry sump engine was sold to F.A. Rhodes, a great Aston fancier who owned in turn almost every pre-war model. In the late thirties another owner fitted this car with a 2 litre six cylinder Scott engine but the ground clearance was minimal and it was discarded.

Oddly enough the 2 seater sports model exhibited at Olympia in 1928 not only had a wet sump engine but also reverted to fixed wings.

The second of the 1928 team cars (LM 2), rebuilt with cycle wings and inside exhaust, was featured in the firm's advertising and was obviously the forerunner of the forthcoming International 2/4 seater.

To blow or not to blow
SUPERCHARGED ASTONS, FACT & FICTION

The late twenties and early thirties was a period of technical innovation for many manufacturers. Small sixes, front wheel drive, superchargers, all had their adherents and at the time of the 1928 Motor Show, Aston Martins boldly denounced all three in a full page advertisement in *The Autocar*. At the same time in an odd about-face they exhibited on their stand at Olympia a standard sports engine fitted with one of George Eyston's 'Powerplus' blowers. As Eyston had been a member of the A.M. works team at Le Mans, there was probably more in this than met the eye.

Nothing further was heard of this project but a year later the Aston catalogue contained details of a supercharged *International* model with a No. 9 'Powerplus' blower mounted between the dumb irons. The chassis price was quoted at £725. A clumsily touched up photograph served to illustrate this phanthom model which like the earlier blown engine was never heard of again, indeed it is doubtful if such a model was ever built.

In the Winter of 1931 a more realistic experiment was carried out when a works car (LM 6) was fitted with a supercharger, again under the radiator which required the engine to be cranked in an anti-clockwise direction! The installation was carried out for Aston Martins by Birkin and Cowper of Welwyn, who of course had had considerable experience in this field with the Blower Bentleys. Nevertheless this blown Aston was not a success and Bertelli never again played around with forced induction. A pity, if only from an aesthetic viewpoint, for this blown car looked really exciting. Unfortunately no photograph is known to exist.

Unsupercharged for efficiency!

The blown engine built as a Show exhibit had a chain driven Powerplus supercharger mounted on the off-side of the engine. There is no record of it having been run.

Racing continues

THE 1929 WORKS' CARS

For the 1929 season the works prepared two cars, LM 2 which had been run at Le Mans the previous year and now carried a 2/4 seater body and LM 3, a new two seater which was more functional than beautiful. The spare wheel was carried horizontally in an exposed position on top of the long pointed tail. A detachable panel over the scuttle, but separate from the bonnet, gave ready access to the back of the instrument panel, a practical innovation.

Considerable efforts were made to reduce the weight, the chassis being extensively drilled and aluminium used for many components including the carburettor bodies. Driven by A.C. Bertelli and Jack Bezzant, the works' foreman, the new car ran fifth in the *J.C.C. Double Twelve Hour Race* at Brooklands and thus made history as the first Feltham built Aston to finish a major event. The second car retired early with a broken connecting rod.

Giving Le Mans a miss the works then entered LM 3 for the *Irish Grand Prix*, which despite its title was a sports car race run in Belfast's Phoenix Park. Regulations for this event called for a two seater body with ballast taking the place of the passenger. This dead weight had to be carried above the chassis frame behind the seats, a ruling to which Bertelli objected, maintaining that it would 'totally spoil the balance of the car which is designed to balance nicely with the passengers'. After protracted correspondence the Royal Irish Automobile Club 'bent' the rules sufficiently to permit the ballast to be divided between the statuary position behind the seats and across the front dumb irons ahead of the radiator. Bertelli and Bezzant finished in 9th place, the latter driver then taking the car to Ulster for the *Tourist Trophy*.

Right at the start of the race Bezzant lost some time by running into the ditch after which the car ran consistently but was not placed.

The car was then re-vamped with a very pretty and original round tailed body and used as demonstrator. Replicas were subsequently marketed as the *International* 2 seater at £598.

The long tailed 1929 works' car (LM 3) during practise for the Junior Car Club's 'Double Twelve' at Brooklands.

Jack Bezzant's unfortunate mishap directly after the start of the 1929 Tourist Trophy race enables one to see quite clearly the arbitary ballast carried in front of the radiator.

A finalised design

THE INTERNATIONAL CHASSIS

After two seasons of racing his low chassis, dry sump engined cars, Bertelli was ready by the 1929 Motor Show to display the true *International* production model so named because it complied with the IARAC regulations and, in theory at least, was sold ready to race.

The beautifully prepared show chassis displayed to advantage all the distinctive Aston Martin features, the single overhead camshaft engine, the separate gearbox, the worm drive axle with its large oil chambers each side of the differential, and the massive rod operated brakes.

In appraising the chassis it is as well to remember that unlike the majority of the smaller manufacturers at that time, Aston Martin utilised very few bought out parts, the only major proprietary units being the newly introduced Bishop steering box (previously used only on commercial vehicles) and the American Borg and Beck single plate clutch.

The show chassis, which was to grace the firm's stand at Olympia for three years, had pale green side members and its numerous aluminium castings were sand blasted to a matt finish contrasting with chrome plated steel and brass components. With the introduction of the 'new' *International* in 1932 it was dismantled and the various parts distributed around the works' stores which accounts for the curiosity aroused in different owners who on ordering spares, received items beautifully buffed and polished.

Preparing a chassis to such a high standard of show finish was of course a costly business even though it was chiefly the work of apprentices (including the writer) and Aston Martin never again indulged in such extravagance.

The polished International chassis, pride of the Aston Martin stand at Olympia in 1929, 1930 and 1931.

The four speed 'crash' gearbox was mounted well back in the frame on three Silentbloc bushes.

Front suspension details showing the short stiff springs and brake torque resisting cables.

The worm drive rear axle proved to be the Achilles heel of the International.

Coachwork by E. Bertelli Ltd
THE INTERNATIONAL 2 AND 2/4 SEATERS

Alongside the stripped chassis at the 1929 Show, pride of place was shared by a delightful little two seater of which only some half dozen were built, and the *International* 2/4 seater, a model which did so much to re-establish the name of Aston Martin. Both bodies were superbly built and finished as indeed were all the products of Harry Bertelli who, although still occupying the 'end shop' as the coachbuilding section at Feltham was always known, was now operating as a separate company, E. Bertelli Ltd. Under this new arrangement they were free to produce coachwork to individual order on both Aston Martin and other makes of chassis and over the years several beautiful Alvis, Riley, Bentley and other cars were to emerge from their works. Harry Bertelli took everything in his stride from a special racing shell for Widengren's Amilcar to a series of spacious all-weather bodies on the larger Vauxhalls. He was also responsible for both the chassis modifications and coachwork of the Graham British Special, surely the most attractive of all the Anglo-American bastards? Both the *International* Astons cost £598, £80 more than the bare chassis, and were covered by a unique guarantee which covered the first owner against all repairs and replacements AT ANY TIME DURING THE LIFE OF THE CAR. The Bertelli brothers were no fools, they knew full well that any major defect in either chassis or body was almost certain to show up during the first twelve months anyway!

A pair of 1929 models at Olympia.

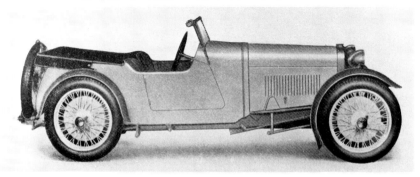

The International 2/4 seater was exhibited for the first time in 1929. It was a model which really established the Feltham Aston Martin as a classic design.

The distinctive and attractive tail of the 2 seater.

Beauty and the beast

TWO SPECIAL ONE-OFF COUPES

In order to rationalise production the *T* type models with upswept frames were discontinued early in 1930 (but a dozen or more frames remained stacked in a corner of the works for several years) and an extended version of the *International* chassis introduced which unlike the previous long chassis used the dry sump engine.

Oddly enough the first of these 9' 6" wheelbase chassis was bodied by an outside coachbuilder, the little known London firm of Harrison & Sons who perpetrated what was surely the dullest car ever to bear the name Aston Martin. It is not knwon who ordered or first owned this ugly fabirc 2/4 seater coupe but when purchased by the author in 1958 (in one of his more impecunious moments) it was on its last legs with water pouring through the sunshine roof in wet weather and seeping through its porous block at all times. It was passed on to an equally impecunious enthusiast who paid a meagre deposit and disappeared. Neither he nor the wretched car were ever seen again.

In direct contrast to the Harrison coupé was a truly magnificent coachbuilt fixed head coupé on the short chassis built to the order of Whitby shipowner W. Headlam. This one-off special was perfectly proportioned with a long bonnet extending beyond the bulkhead. Finished in black cellulose with a chromium strip at waist level its flowing lines emphasised the skill and craftsmanship of the pre-war panel beater at his best.

A year or so later Headlam had the engine bored out to 1750 cc and the coupé became the first '2 litre' Aston Martin with a maximum speed approaching 100 mph which causes one to ponder with Le Mans in mind!

Possibly the most beautiful of all pre-war Astons was this one-off coupé by Bertelli built to the order of Whitby ship owner, W.S. Headlam.

Definitely the most ugly was this coupé on the long chassis built by the little known London firm of Harrison and Sons.

A third racing season

THE 1930 WORKS' CARS

For 1930 the works prepared two racing cars, a completely new one, LM 4 and old LM 3 with a new two seater body (again with exposed spare wheel on top of the tail) replacing the standard two seater it had been wearing during the winter spent as work's demonstrator. This was the third completely different body carried by this car which serves to indicate the problems facing the motor historian when he comes to sort out which particular car ran in which race and who were the individual drivers.

The new car had a body closely following the lines of the *International* 2 seater but without doors. Both racers had shortened cycle wings with the exhausts leading down from standard manifolds inside the bonnets. Altogether an attractive, tidy pair of cars forming the most business-like equipe to emerge from Feltham up to that time. They ran in the *Double Twelve*, where Bertelli and Nigel Holder finished in fourth place with the new car at an average speed of 73,76 mph, and at Phoenix Park where both cars finished, Sammy Davis driving LM 4 into 7th place, the highest placed 1½ litre. Bertelli was 15th.

Back at the works after the 1930 'Double Twelve', LM 4 still carries the mud and grime of 24 hours racing at Brooklands.

Bertelli and mechanic 'Auburn' seated in the re-bodied LM 3 before the start of the 1930 Irish Grand Prix.

Amateur racer

A BARKER BODIED 2 SEATER

Harry Bertelli's bodies, which he drew full size on an outsize blackboard on the wall of the body shop, were so 'right' in their purity of line and so fittingly proportioned in relation to his brother's chassis that few customers had reason to order special one-off designs either from the works or from outside specialists. To the majority of those fortunate enough to afford an Aston Martin at all, the very fact of ownership of such a costly, exclusive car established their individuality. But, nevertheless as we have seen, there was the occasional client who wished to exercise a spot of one-upmanship and for them a stripped chassis was available at £550 supplied complete with bonnet, dumb iron apron and Aston's own distinctive cycle wings.

The first short chassis ordered individually was purchased by amateur racing driver H.S. Eaton, who had been one of Bamford and Martin's early clients and now commissioned Barker and Company of South Audley Street to design and build a doorless two seater racing shell for road events. It was quite an attractive little body with deep cut away sides but one would have thought not sufficiently different to the standard two seater to warrant the additional expense.

Eaton raced the car only once, in the *Irish Grand Prix* in 1930 when he was co-opted into the work's team of two cars, Bertelli having his eye on the team prize. Unfortunately the owner-driver considered the car too highly geared for the circuit and after 16 laps retired. There followed heated discussions at the pits but no amount of persuasion would make him continue and so any possible chance of the team prize was lost for good.

H.S. Eaton's special Barker bodied 2 seater.

Eaton at Phoenix Park before his controversial retirement.

One man's meat

LONG CHASSIS MODELS FOR 1930

Exhibited at Olympia in 1930 were two new body styles on the long chassis which attracted a good deal of comment. These comprised a four door tourer and what was designated the *Sportsman's Coupé*, a design that might appear somewhat ungainly and boxy to modern eyes, but was of a current fashionable style and was undoubtedly a splendid example of Harry Bertelli's versatility and the craftsmanship of his men. The interior was upholstered in pig skin accentuating the general air of elegance reflected externally by the handsome thermostatically controlled radiator shutters and the costly hand louvred valance concealing the chassis frame and brake rods. Listed at an extravagant £750, only three examples were built, the most striking being a bright yellow version with black wings specially made for Percy Kidner who had but recently joined the board of Aston Martin Ltd.

The four door tourer was also attractive in an odd chunky sort of way. In this model the cycle pattern wings were abandoned in favour of a stylish swept variety. No running boards were fitted the frame being concealed by plain valances. It was a roomy body in which the designer cleverly camouflaged its length by mounting the wide doors at a rearwards sloping angle. At £650 it was considerably cheaper than the *Sportsman's Coupé* which remained the most expensive 1½ litre ever offered by the Feltham concern.

Not everyone's cup of tea perhaps, but undeniably a fine example of Harry Bertelli's craftsmanship was the International Sportsman's coupé.

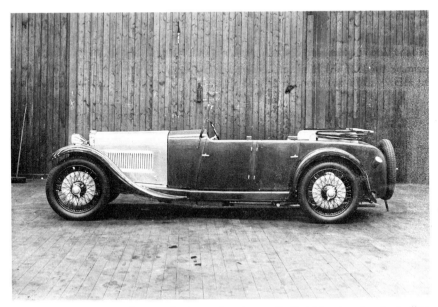

A four seater tourer, also on the long chassis, awaits finishing touches including the fitting of the hood envelope.

One upmanship

TWO BODIES BY OUTSIDE COACHBUILDERS

During the summer of 1930 two further special bodied cars were built both quite distinctive in their own way and different from anything in the catalogued range.

The first was a 2/3 seater drop head coupé on the short chassis by James Young of Bromley, a concern well known for their sporting coachwork on Alfa-Romeos. This particular Aston was fabric covered with squarish boot, cycle wings and unvalanced frame. A two branch exhaust led from the side of the bonnet which was fabric covered except for the louvred panel on each side. The radiator was embellished with one of the mesh stone guards which were an optional extra fitted to only a small number of *Internationals*.

The second special job was also in fabric, built on the Weymann principle. This was a two door saloon mounted on the long wheel base chassis by Messrs Freestone and Webb of Willesden for Kensington-Moir and Straker, probably to celebrate their appointment as Aston Martin distributors. Freestone and Webb were of course renowned for big luxury saloons on Bentley, Mercedes and other powerful chassis, so it is perhaps not surprising that their flirtation with a chassis as small as the 1½ litre Aston did not match their more exotic creations but nevertheless, the resulting design was distinctly pleasing. Regrettably it appears to have been broken up many years ago.

This pretty little coupe by James Young of Bromley must surely have met with the generous approval of Harry Bertelli.

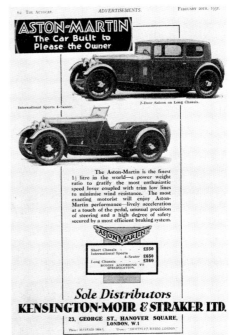

Messrs Kensington-Moir & Straker, the Aston Martin distributors in 1931, featured their own Freestone and Webb fabric saloon in their advertising.

A desperate gamble

THE 1931 WORKS' CARS

By the winter of 1930-1931 the world slump had really set in
and Aston Martins by the very nature of their business were sorely
hit. Fortunately Bertelli's personal reputation throughout the
trade was of such high standing that his various suppliers volun-
teered long term credit and the late H.J. Aldington of Frazer
Nash cars, a wealthy man in his own right, came up with a
temporary rescue operation which included the financing, building
and running of a team of no less than three cars for the 1931
season. At first Bertelli was reluctant to accept such aid, but work
had already been started on the racers and he realised that this
could well be the end of the road for Aston Martins, so he took a
gamble and mortgaged the whole outfit to Aldington who thereby
became the official entrant in the *Double Twelve* of three Aston
Martins in addition to three Frazer Nash.

The three new A.M.s, numbered LM5, 6 and 7, were the most
highly developed *Internationals* built, delivering 70 bhp. With
lowered radiators, drooping tails and large cowled scuttles, they
were not the most handsome of Bertelli's racers but they certainly
looked the part and were quite fast, being timed at 95 mph down
Newtownards Straight in the *T.T.* They also ran at Le Mans where
Bertelli qualified for the final of the *Rudge Cup* the following
year. The other two cars were troubled with fracturing of
bolts securing wings and lamps, a problem that was to plague the
marque through several seasons.

In the *Tourist Trophy* in Ulster, C.M. Harvey was first in Class F,
which combined with the *Rudge Cup* qualification certainly made
Bertelli's gamble worthwhile for L. Prideaux-Brune was sufficient-

ly impressed to inject fresh finance into the firm which enabled them to pay off H.J. Aldington and continue production on a limited scale.

K.S. Peacock with works' foreman Jim Smith, before the weighing in at Le Mans in 1931.

Following breakage of wing stays at Le Mans in 1931, the team cars were modified for the TT with front wings mounted on massive cross tubes. The drivers for Ulster (left to right) were H.W. Cook, A.C. Bertelli and the late Major C.M. Harvey.

Old soldiers never die

THE 1931 TEAM IN LATER YEARS

At the close of the 1931 racing season the three works' cars went their different ways and today, in common with all but one of the Feltham pre-war team cars they have survived, which is proof of the ruggedness and durability of the little 1½ litre Aston Martin and its unique dry sump engine.

LM5 was run in the 1933 *RAC Rally* by B. Crosthwaite for which event it was fitted with a special four seater body with external rear fuel tank, similar to the later *Le Mans* models. The second car, LM6 was for two years the works guinea pig and was used in abortive supercharger experiments as described on page 82. In unblown form it was loaned to Swedish driver H. Widengren for the *Swedish Winter Grand Prix* in which he came 9th. Later it was purchased by Mr and Mrs G.S. White who raced it at Brooklands, Brighton and Shelsley Walsh. Thirty years later, Roy Dudley restored it to mint condition and proudly drove it into first place in the 1967 St. John Horsfall race at Silverstone.

The third car of the team, LM7, which had been the least successful during the season, was purchased by the young amateur driver Mortimer Morris-Goodall, who immediately embarked upon an extensive and varied competition programme. He drove the car in all the major trials, the L.C.C. Relay Race and the J.C.C. 1000 Miles Race at Brooklands as well as many smaller events. In 1933 he was co-opted into the works' team for Le Mans where LM7 ran for a second time, a distinction bestowed on few cars in the history of that great race.

Then as Morris-Goodall progressed into the top class, his old car passed into the hands of others and became butchered and neglected. Happily in recent years it has been restored by the author and Les Wigmore to almost original condition apart from the substitution of a later *Le Mans* rear axle in place of the original worm drive.

LM 5 with 2/4 seater body and slab tank. In this form it ran in the 1933 RAC Hastings Rally driven by B. Crosthwaite.

Still racing in 1967, LM 6 won the A.M.O.C. St. John Horsfall Trophy Race driven by its restorer Roy Dudley and, as seen here, was also a formidable concours contestant.

In 1970, LM 7 was rebuilt by the author with the assistance of Les Wigmore.

Change for the sake of change

A NEW 2 SEATER INTERNATIONAL

Perhaps for no other reason than that of change, the delightful little rounded tail *International* 2 seater was replaced at the time of the 1931 Show by the *Le Mans* 2 seater which in effect was a production replica of the team cars with the same drooping tail and exaggerated scuttle cowls. It was a shade longer than its predecessor and being intended as a practical road going car, luggage space was provided in the tail by mounting the spare wheel externally just ahead of the off side front door, but at least one owner found the luggage space too limited for extensive touring. Unusual was the contoured bench style seat, a curious innovation in such a sporting vehicle. The catalogue price was £650. Five examples were built but only one, originally owned by G.F.A. Manby-Colegrave, is believed to survive. For an additional £50 a *Le Mans* engine was available with high lift camshaft and 'special tuning'.

One of these *Le Mans* 2 seaters, finished in two shades of blue was supplied to the special order of racing driver W.A. Cuthbert who had the gear and brake levers fitted on the right hand side outside the body, the gear lever protruding through a dummy door which must have horrified the artistic eye of Harry Bertelli, but then the customer is always right! This car was almost completely wrecked on its first outing and after being rebuilt appeared in some minor Brooklands handicap events with little success. Bertelli's cars were always too heavy and lacking in acceleration for this kind of competition.

The Le Mans 2 seater introduced in 1931 was a close replica of the works' team cars, this particular example being supplied by the Birmingham distributors Patrick Motors Ltd, to Mr F.J. Trentham of Knowle.

W.A. Cuthbert's similar model had the seldom exercised optional right-hand control levers. How Harry Bertelli must have hated that dummy door, but the customer is always right!

The same but different

TWO SPECIALS ON A SIMILAR THEME

A visitor to the 1931 Motor Show was the late George Hartwell, an amateur racing driver who ran a sports car business at Oxford, catering, no doubt, to the young University bloods. Hartwell was rather taken by the Aston Martin *Le Mans* 2 seater and visualised a four seater on the same lines and ordered such a car which was illustrated in *The Autocar* and announced as the *Le Mans* 2/4 seater sports at £675. In actual fact it never appeared in the firm's catalogue being superseded the following year by the 'real' *Le Mans* models with unit gearbox and bevel rear axle.

Today Hartwell's unique car is owned by Mr C. Black to whom the original owner wrote shortly before his death in 1970, relating how the car came to be built 'the car is a one-off and originally came about by my interest in the Le Mans Replica two seater which was the centre piece of the Aston Martin stand at the 1931 Motor Show. However, although the car appealed to me tremendously, my requirement was for what is now known as a 2+2 and I suggested to A.C. Bertelli that the body style of the 100 mph Invicta would suit my requirements. As a result it was decided to build a car for me on the Le Mans Replica chassis with the coachwork up to the rear of the front seats as per the two seater model and the rear end to be copied as near as possible from the Invicta. After the Show the Bertelli brothers drew out full size the side and rear elevation at their factory, which satisfied me and the car was produced'.

Around the same time the comedian Jimmy Nervo who owned one of the *Le Mans* 2 seaters had similar ideas to Hartwell, for whilst he was delighted with the car's performance characteristics for commuting between London and the provincial music halls, he had become frustrated with the limited luggage accomodation. In answer to his problems he discarded the original body and commissioned Messrs Freestone and Webb to build a new 2/4 seater which, by accident or design, was almost identical to Hartwell's and oddly enough was even more Invicta-like, for the central filler spout on the rear tank was set rearwards at a slight angle exactly like the Invicta.

The comedian Nervo of 'Nervo and Knox' replaced his Le Mans 2 seater body with a 2/4 seater with outside tank, the work being carried out by Freestone and Webb.

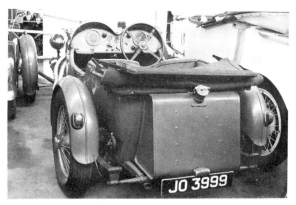

The rear end of the Invicta inspired Le Mans 2/4 seater built at the works for the late George Hartwell. Now the property of C.H.I. Black.

For doctors and rally drivers
THE INTERNATIONAL DROPHEAD COUPE

The use of running boards was a distinctly unusual departure for
E. Bertelli Ltd who built this pretty little drophead coupé on the
short chassis to the order of L. Prideaux-Brune, who drove it in
the 1932 *RAC Rally* and thereby initiated a long personal
association with the marque. He was for a short time a director of
the company and for many years his Winter Garden Garage in
Drury Lane were London distributors. A second similar coupé was
exhibited at the 1931 Motor Show and catalogued at £715, but no
further examples were built. The show model differed from
Prideaux-Brune's in minor details. It had external hood irons and
the front wings flowed in a more gentle curve to the running
boards.

Sadly neither coupé has survived in its original form. The rally car
was discovered some years ago in a pitiful state and subsequently
rebuilt as an open model, the drophead body being beyond
restoration. It is unfortunate that few of the less sporting vintage
Astons remain intact, the majority, particularly the long chassis
models, having been broken up and used as spares in the preser-
vation of the remaining sports cars.

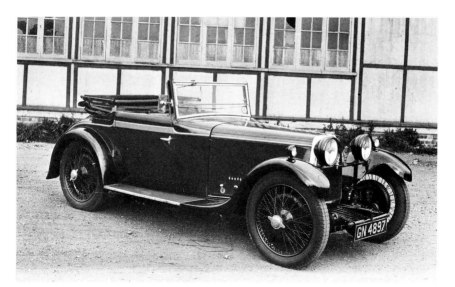

Lea-Francis or Swift would have described this body style as a 'Doctor's Coupé' but to Lance Prideaux-Brune it was eminently suited for competing in the RAC Rally.

Like so many of the less sporting Aston Martins of the mid-thirties, Prideaux-Brune's coupe obviously passed into unappreciative hands and in 1955 was discovered in this sorry state.

Family favourites

LONG CHASSIS SALOONS

The squarish *Sportsman's Coupé* having met with some sales resistance its place at Olympia in 1931, was taken by a very handsome four door saloon together with a two door version. Both models had flowing front wings, inswept just ahead of the door, with a valanced chassis frame completing a generally tidy appearance. At the rear an integral trunk, fabric covered on the two door model, carried the spare wheel vertically on the back which opened on a side hinge.

In common with all Bertelli bodies they were beautifully made, framed in 'best quality ash' and panelled in aluminium. Upholstery was in hide or Bedford cloth to choice. Safety glass was fitted all round with wind-up windows in the doors and a small opening glass panel in the roof. Equipment was luxurious embracing two interior lights, companions, two dash lamps, speedometer, eight-day clock, fuel gauge, oil pressure gauge, ammeter and radiator thermometer. The comprehensive kit of good quality tools included special rocker spanners, camshaft sprocket retaining cup for maintaining correct timing when removing the head, and an oddly shaped plug spanner necessary in order to reach the somewhat inaccessible rear plugs.

The cars were supplied in any colour desired. Only the one two door saloon was built and a mere half dozen of the four door versions. The two door car was listed at £725, the four door costing an extra £20. The four door tourer was still available but it is probable that these were remaining stock.

'The nicest car in the Show' was how The Light Car and Cyclecar described the handsome four door saloon on the long chassis.

Equally attractive was the two door version of which only one was built.

The end of a classic
THE LAST INTERNATIONAL 2/4 SEATER

The last 'real' *International* 2/4 seater with separate gearbox and worm drive axle was completed at Feltham in January 1932 immediately prior to the introduction of the *New International* with unit gearbox, cable brakes and bevel drive. It is as well therefore that we take a final look at the Bertelli brothers' joint masterpiece which has become one of the classic sports cars of all time.

In appearance these last *Internationals* differed hardly at all from the first 2/4 seater of 1929 which shows how right it was in the first place. Most noticeable changes were a slightly taller radiator, wider rear seat, tidier division between bonnet and scuttle and a change in the angle of the hood when furled. Mechanical differences were more numerous but mostly of a minor nature. The brakes had been revised with the adoption of wider drums and shoes with dual fulcrums as used on the 1931 team cars and, also a racing development, torque stays on the front axle were fitted to counteract brake reaction. The worm drive axle, always the Achilles heel of this model, had been progressively beefed up but remained a fragile component to the very end and no one was sorry to see it go.

Although a pretty car by any standards, the *International* was also extremely rugged and therefore heavy which meant it was lacking in acceleration and maximum speed in comparison with its immediate rivals. It was also very, very expensive. So what then compelled more than seventy enthusiasts to purchase such a car at such a time? Contemporary road tests provide the answer as exemplified by *The Motor* who said 'There are faster cars, there are more lively cars but when all is said and done, it is the average speed that counts. The Aston Martin without being driven at more than 70 mph maximum will put up averages over a run of 150 · miles or so that most people who do not know the car would believe impossible'.

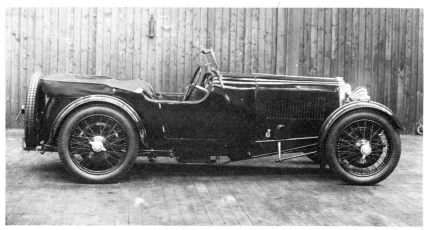

To a great many enthusiasts the lines of the International 2/4 seater remain unsurpassed.

A.C. Bertelli's personal International had a specially length-ened gear lever probably necessitated by an injury to his left hand as the result of an accident with a 30/98 Vauxhall many years before.

An Aston for £475!
THE NEW INTERNATIONAL

Having barely completed expensive chassis jigs to facilitate series
production of the short chassis, Bertelli and his new financial
backer, Lance Prideaux-Brune, had a complete re-think and in a
determined effort to cut costs came out with a revised design,
incorporating two major bought out components, a Moss gearbox mounted in unit with the engine and an E.N.V. bevel
gear rear axle with open propshaft. At the same time new
frame members, still underslung at the rear, remained parallel from
the dash rearwards which made for easier machining. The
splendid A.M. brakes were retained but the expensive and
complicated rod operation was discarded in favour of enclosed
cables. The handbrake lever was moved to the outside of the
frame on the driver's right hand. The dry sump engine now had
the dynamo driven directly off the front of the crankshaft and
the magneto was moved forward to a position immediately
behind the water pump.

These changes were made at the beginning of 1932 and initially
the familiar 2/4 seater sports body was continued on this chassis
but for some reason difficult to determine, the complete car
lacked the aesthetic balance of the previous *International*, possibly
due to the taller radiator combined with the impression of a wider
track caused by the elimination of the Perrot brake gear.

Despite a considerable price reduction of £120, only twelve
examples were sold before the introduction of the low radiator
Le Mans model later in the season.

A new angular winged badge picked out in cream enamel

(designed by Sammy Davis) distinguished the new tall radiator models from the earlier cars.

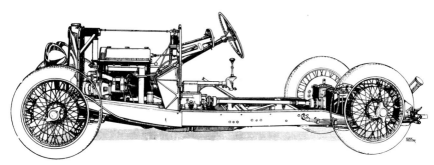

The new International chassis pictured by the late Max Millar of The Autocar who spent two whole days at the works, sat on an up-turned crate with his drawing board across his knees.

The new International 2/4 seater broadly followed the lines of its predecessor but the taller radiator and revised braking system made it less attractive from this angle.

At last a major success

THE 1932 WORKS' CARS

With the backing of L. Prideaux-Brune, Bertelli was once again able to build a full team of three cars for the 1932 season but their assembly was late in starting and preliminary tests were carried out during the three days preceding the *J.C.C. 1000 Miles Race* (a two day affair replacing the *Double Twelve* of previous years). During these tests trouble was experienced with the front suspension and the cars were withdrawn from the Brooklands race as Le Mans followed only two weeks later. With stiffer front springs the three cars were in fine fettle for Le Mans, where Bertelli with co-driver L.P. Driscoll won the *Rudge-Whitworth Bienniel Cup* at an average speed of 58.7 mph, the first really great international success for the marque and one that did not receive the recognition it warranted. In fact it took six months to get the Cup out of customs! They were seventh in general classification with Newsome and Widengren doing even better with 5th position at 62 mph although not eligible for the Rudge Cup.

Numbered LM8, 9 and 10, these cars, based on the new *International* chassis, differed considerably in appearance from any previous Aston Martin, having small sharply V-fronted radiators, the bonnets just clearing the top of the engine. The low built bodies with flat scuttles and grand prix style tails looked really splendid although the general ensemble was again marred by mounting the wings on crudely fashioned blacksmith's stays braced by steel cables ... Bertelli had not forgotten the debacle caused by the shedding of wings the previous year. Yet even so the Cup winner finished with rope lashed from the front wings to the windscreen supports!

The following week-end Bertelli, passengered by Widengren, made a demonstration climb at Shelsley Walsh using an 8 to 1 bottom gear.

LM8 was then sold to the work's service manager, C.H. Wood, who changed the body to a four seater; LM9 was sold to S.H. Grylls who many years later was to achieve fame as designer of the Rolls-Royce 'Silver Shadow'. R.A. Slay, a director of Squire Motors, acquired LM10 but ran it for only a short while before selling it back to the works for use as a development vehicle.

H.S. Peacock in one of the new low radiatored team cars at the weighing-in at Le Mans in 1932.

A pit scene during Le Mans practise in 1932 with Team Manager 'Sammy' Davis and works' foreman Jim Smith in attendance.

Marking time

ONE-OFF BODIES DURING WORKS' RE-ORGANISATION

After the Le Mans race, a couple of 2 seater sports models with low radiators were laid down but never catalogued as standard models. In appearance they were similar to the work's cars but with flared scuttles and full cycle wings. They have since become known as the *Competition* two seaters.

Otherwise the factory was almost idle going through a period of re-organisation with merely a handful of the new *Internationals* being assembled. These included a rather special version for a Mr G.H. Fisher, who specified a flared scuttle and rear slab tank rather like the one supplied to G.R. Hartwell on the earlier chassis. A body of similar style but of much lower build was fitted to one of the team cars, LM8, and supplied to C.H. Wood. The surplus racing body was then fitted to a new chassis and raced by R.O. Shuttleworth in the Tourist Trophy after which the car was rebuilt with a tall radiator and standard 2/4 seater body for a subsequent owner who desired a car with a racing history combined with the comfort and convenience of a touring car. LM8 in 2/4 seater form was illustrated in an advertisement for E. Bertelli Ltd (the only time they ever advertised) which suggests it might have been the true prototype for the forthcoming *Le Mans* 2/4 seater.

Taken at Brooklands this photo shows one of the rare Competition 2 seaters owned at that time by Miss Betty Haig.

Built to the order of G.H. Fisher, this special bodied new International was very similar to the earlier Le Mans 2/4 seater built for the late George Hartwell.

In their sole venture into advertising, E. Bertelli Ltd used an illustration of the 1932 ex-works car, LM 8, fitted with a 2/4 seater body which foreshadowed the Le Mans 2/4 seater production models.

White elephants

THE 12/50 SALOON AND TOURER

Having cut the cost of their short chassis by more than £100, Aston Martins thought they would have another try at a tempting market which they had never successfully breached, a long chassis (10' wheelbase) mounted with more practical tourer and saloon coachwork for a less sporting clientele. In theory this would seem to have been a sound proposition, particularly in view of the substantial reduction in the cost of the chassis but, the resultant body styles could only have been designed by Harry Bertelli in one of his less inspired moments.

The saloon, in particular, lacked the elegant lines of the earlier *International* saloon and the tourer with only two doors was little better although the hood, now folding down inside the body, gave a tidier appearance than hitherto.

Named the *12/50* or *Standard*, only about twenty were built all told and the distributors had the greatest difficulty in selling even that number. The cars were shuffled around between the various agents, Winter Garden in London, Hartwells of Oxford, Grosvenor Garage in Manchester, Cresta Motors of Worthing and Patrick Motors of Birmingham. Some of the saloons were even returned to the works, re-sprayed in different colours and replaced in the showrooms thus creating the impression that a car had been sold and replaced with fresh stock. The last long chassis model, a tourer, was sold in May 1935, 2½ years after it had been built!

Additionally two of these touring chassis were fitted with rudimentary open truck bodies and employed as work's transport. Disguised as team tenders they were taken to Le Mans thus ensuring an adequate supply of spares on a simplified 'carnet'.

Dull in both appearance and performance the 12/50 Saloon of 1932 was mounted on a long wheel base version of the new International chassis.

The 12/50 Tourer also on the long chassis, was better looking than the saloon but was an equally poor seller.

New appearance, new performance
THE LE MANS 2/4 SEATER

Unveiled at Olympia in October 1932, the *Le Mans* 2/4 seater replaced the famous *International* and was an immediate success setting a new high in Aston Martin production figures. Almost one hundred examples being produced within twelve months. Whether this was due to the marque's success at Le Mans, the improved economic climate, the virtual take over of the concern by Sir Arthur Sutherland and his son, the vigorous sales drive of L. Prideaux-Brune at his new Winter Garden Garage or simply to the excellence of the new model is hard to determine. Probably it was a combination of all these factors.

Certainly the new car was the finest Aston Martin to emanate from Feltham up to that time, indeed to many enthusiasts it remains the finest of them all. It was a rugged, yet very pretty motor car and although carrying 2/4 seater coachwork, it bore an exciting resemblance to the cars that had achieved victory at Le Mans. The hood folding down inside the body added to the neat appearance and the outside exhausts with Brooklands silencer were a distinctive feature as were the inevitable cycle wings which had become almost an A.M. trade mark. These wings must have been 'cheaper by the dozen' for they were delivered regularly to the works in quantities far outstripping the number of cars produced and were stacked in vast piles outside the stores. Today they are worth their weight in gold!

Early *Le Mans* models still featured 21" wheels which made them appear a little spidery but once the model had settled down to a production run, 18" wheels were introduced improving the appearance considerably.

Following their victory in the Rudge-Whitworth Cup at Le Mans in 1932, the new chassis with unit gearbox and cable brakes acquired the low radiator as used on the racers and became the Le Mans model.

Built in larger numbers than any previous Aston Martin model, the Le Mans 2/4 seater was an immediate success. This early example, built for R. Gordon Sutherland soon after his father took control of the company, had 21" wheels. Later production models had 18" wheels which improved the car's appearance considerably.

For the sporting family

THE LE MANS SPECIAL 4 SEATER

Despite the dismal sales record of the *12/50* saloons and tourers, the Aston Martin directors still sought a market for a full four seater and in conjunction with Winter Garden Garage indulged in a mild form of market research. Their findings suggested that there were indeed prospective customers for whom the name Aston Martin and the quality it had come to represent had a strong appeal but who found the sports models too sporty and impractical for their requirements and the existing long chassis models not sporting enough.

The compromise answer to such a demand was met with the *Le Mans Special*, a full four seater open model on an extended version of the *Le Mans* chassis. With its squat radiator, low build, outside exhausts and cycle wings it was every inch of its ten foot wheelbase a real Aston Martin in appearance yet seating four people in reasonable comfort (its passengers ahead of the rear axle) and having good luggage accomodation in the attractive tail. They cost £625 when they were introduced at the 1933 Show and sold quite well with some fifteen or sixteen being built over a period of six months.

Unfortunately like all the long chassis pre-war Astons, they were a trifle unwieldly and the frames were inclined to whip with the result that in time the tails would break away, the aluminium panels splitting just ahead of the boot. Few have survived, present day enthusiasts finding them a good source of spares for their sports models which still exist in such considerable numbers.

Introduced at Olympia in 1933 a 9' 10" wheelbase sports chassis was made available with full four seater coachwork and named the Le Mans Special. Unlike the later long chassis Mark II it never appeared in saloon form.

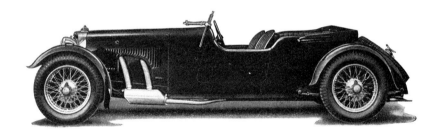

To beg, borrow or steal

THE 1933 WORKS' TEAM

Early in 1933 financial control of Aston Martins passed into the hands of Sir Arthur Sutherland K.B.E., whose son Gordon became Joint Managing Director with Bertelli.

Sir Arthur Sutherland never did share his son's enthusiasm for motor racing and, perhaps wisely, was anxious to see the new *Le Mans* models placed on a proper production basis before sanctioning the building of any new racing cars and in any case, it was a bit late to embark on such a project for the coming season. So for the first time in six years, Bertelli was unable to build at least one new racer, but he was determined not to be robbed of his annual excursion to Le Mans. He and Gordon Sutherland scraped together a rather motley team of cars for this one race, in which, as things turned out, they did rather well.

The team of three cars was made up of LM10, the works' development car, LM9, loaned by its owner S.H. Grylls, and Morris-Goodall's veteran 1931 team car, LM7. The works' car was allocated to Bertelli himself and Sammy Davis who was making a return to the wheel of a racing car after his nasty accident in an Invicta at the 1931 Brooklands Easter Meeting. They eventually finished 7th overall, 2nd in class and 4th in the Rudge Cup. The second car was driven by Pat Driscoll and C. Penn Hughes who were 5th at 66,3 mph, faster than the marque's best performance the previous year. They were also first in their class and 2nd in the Rudge Cup. Morris-Goodall drove his own car with Mrs Elsie Wisdom, but after running in 10th place they were unfortunate in having a main bearing collapse and were forced to retire.

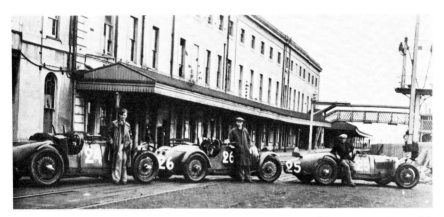

The 1933 works' team for Le Mans comprised two 1932 cars together with Morris-Goodall's 1931 car (centre). This rather mixed bag is seen en route for Le Mans.

The re-built 1932 cars are seen here with Morris-Goodall and A.C. Bertelli. The works in the background are those of Aston Martin's neighbours, the Union Construction Company, builders of London's famous Feltham tram cars.

A new team once more

THE 1934 WORKS' CARS

After an exceedingly successful 1933 Olympia Show with sales far better than anything the company had experienced previously, Bertelli and Gordon Sutherland deemed the time was ripe to think of building a new team for Le Mans once more and three new cars were laid down numbered LM11, 12 and 14. The number 13 was omitted in deference to Bertelli's superstition.

The new cars had very slim bodies with unusual tails which broadened out at the base to conceal the spare wheel carried horizontally at chassis level behind the fuel tank. Mechanically they were a development of the *Le Mans* model being in effect prototypes of the Mark II destined for introduction the following spring. They had drilled frames and were lightened considerably in other directions making them ineligible for the *Tourist Trophy* three months after the French race. So for Ulster, LM11 and LM12 were rebuilt with solid frames and a third completely new car, LM17 was constructed. The two rebuilt cars were re-numbered LM15 and LM16. Minor modifications made to conform to the RAC regulations, were the transfer of the side lamps from the scuttle to the front wings which like those at the rear, had to be increased in width by one inch. This was done by riveting an additional strip along the outer edge, an appendage still carried by these cars.

Le Mans that year proved to be Aston's darkest hour for all three cars were put out of the race, two with lubrication problems caused by the dynamo dogs chewing into the aluminium of the front engine casting and the third with the starter immovably and inexplicably engaging with the flywheel.

For the *TT*, Bertelli once more succumbed to superstition and had the cars painted in his own Italian red. That certainly seems to have cast a magic spell for they won the team award, broke the lap record in Class F and finished 3rd, 6th and 7th overall.

The 1934 works' cars used full cycle wings once more which looked much tidier than those used in 1932 and 1933 which can be glimpsed on the right of the picture on the privately entered car of 'Vincent' (R.E. Tongue) and Maurice Falkner. The gentleman leaning on the fence and wearing overall coat is Harry Bertelli, the coachbuilder.

Seen at the docks en route to Ulster are the three works' cars prepared for the 1934 TT.

The last of a line
THE MARK II CHASSIS

In the spring of 1934, much to Prideaux-Brune's annoyance, for he still had a few *Le Mans* models in stock, the *Mark II* was introduced and the 1½ litre Aston Martin entered its final phase, incorporating all that had been proved and tested during the previous year's racing.

The engine had a new counter-balanced crankshaft, modified cylinder head with more efficient combustion chamber, wider timing gears, longer Weller spring and Auto-Klean oil filter which could be cleaned at regular intervals by simply turning a handle on top of the unit.

With a compression ratio of 7.5 to 1, 70 bhp was developed at 5200 rpm, which, as *The Autocar* pointed out, could only be fully appreciated if one was able to follow authenticated data on other engines of similar capacity. Various modifications had also been made to the chassis in order to stiffen the frame and improve road holding. A heavier gauge material was used for the side members and an additional cross member fitted behind the engine. At the same time the front shock absorbers, still of Hartford friction pattern, were mounted transversely resulting in greatly improved front axle behaviour. A strengthened bulkhead also contributed to chassis stiffness.

The stripped chassis complete with the familiar cycle wings was listed at £535 in short 8' 7" or 10' 0" wheelbase versions.

The Mark II chassis was a development of the Le Mans model with more powerful engine and stronger frame.

Visible changes under the bonnet of the Mark II included the 'Auto-Kleen' oil filter and deeper bulk head castings.

Sales appeal
THE MARK II 2/4 SEATER

The standard body style on the short *Mark II* chassis was very similar to the superseded *Le Mans* but with a flat scuttle, which was less expensive to make, a hood that folded outside the body providing more width for the rear seat passengers, and a new practical feature was the fitting of side flaps on the windscreen which could be removed and used as aero screens with the main screen folded flat. The provision of outside door handles met with some criticism from the more sporty types as did the thermostatically controlled radiator shutters. They were thought to indicate a softening of the breed and indeed whether the *Mark II* looked better than the car it replaced remains a matter of opinion, but it certainly proved to be the best selling of all the 1½ litre Astons and did much to consolidate the financial success of the company which had been steadily improving under the commercial acumen of Gordon Sutherland.

The first *Mark II*, a pale blue 2/4 seater, after being driven in the *Scottish Rally* by Mrs Rutherford, was retained by the works for experimental purposes during the course of which it was bored out to 1750 cc when the introduction of the 2 litre was under consideration. In its original form it was tested by *The Autocar* who considered that 'none of the merits of the car has been lost, particularly as regards controllability'. In their tester's hands it attained a maximum speed of 85.71 mph with the screen folded flat.

The first Mark II 2/4 seater, BME 399, photographed in the car park at Dorset House, home of The Autocar, who published the first Road Test of this model.

Known at the works as the 'Blue Car', the prototype Mark II early in its career competed in the RASC Rally driven by Mrs Rutherford. Later it was bored out to 1750 cc when the 2 litre was being hatched.

Variants on a theme

2 SEATERS ON MARK II CHASSIS

As was the case with the *Le Mans* chassis, no open two seater was ever catalogued on the *Mark II* (the *Ulster* being an entirely different kettle of fish) but in response to individual demand four or five such bodies were built by E. Bertelli. All of a similar pattern, they had sloping tails with the spare wheel sunk into the lid of the boot in similar fashion to the rear end of the full four seater *Le Mans Special*. There was also at least one *Mark II* fitted with *Ulster* style body but slightly wider and having doors. And, conversely, one of the 1934 team cars finished up with a 2/5 seater body.

A further two seater emanated from Germany of all places. This was the creation of Glaser Karosserie of Dresden to the order of Werner Hillegaart who raced the car in local sports car events but found the somewhat luxurious coachwork (which retained the familiar A.M. cycle type wings) rather a handicap, so a second lighter body was built for the Eifelrennen sports car events at the Nurburgring but says Hillegaart, 'still it was a bit heavy compared with other competitive cars although it had a splendid engine'.

After the war this highly individual *Mark II* with the original Glaser body found its way back to this country but sadly it has lost its correct wings and outside exhaust. Nevertheless, it remains the only recorded example of a *Mark II* fitted with a body by an outside coachbuilder and the only pre-war car sold overseas in chassis form.

This 2 seater on the Mark II chassis, supplied to R.G. Barlow, was one of a limited number built by E. Bertelli but never catalogued as a production model.

Very much a 'one-off' special was this 2 seater built by Glaser of Dresden for the amateur German driver Werner Hillegaart.

The same car with the light weight racing body used in the Eifelrennen sports car events.

Sporting luxury

THE MARK II SALOON AND 4 SEATER

The *Le Mans Special* four seater having proved to be a commercial proposition, it is not surprising that a long wheel base *Mark II* chassis was quickly introduced in order to provide the basis of a similar model. With a tail treatment identical to the earlier car, it was in all other respects similar to the short 2/4 seater with flat scuttle and hood folding outside the body. On some examples the offside door had a deep cut-away providing increased elbow room for the driver.

With one or two of the dreadful 12/50 saloons still lurking in distributors' showrooms, the manufacturers revised their opinion as to what constituted a sports saloon and Harry Bertelli came up with one of his finest creations, the *Mark II* saloon. Catalogued at £710, it showed a considerable increase on the previous closed car but there was really no way in which the two could be compared. Had the term 'Gran Turismo' been in vogue in the mid-thrities, then the *Mark II* saloon would have merited such a title. It was a close coupled four seater, the passengers sitting ahead of the rear axle, with two wide doors and luxuriously appointed within. Extremely low built, it had a beautiful roof line sweeping down to the tail in which one could place a reasonable amount of baggage. The spare wheel was recessed in the boot lid and there was a sunshine roof.

Weighing no less than 25 cwt with four up it was of course not particularly fast, 76 mph being the claimed maximum, but due to the extra stiffness of the body structure, road holding was better than any of the open cars. At the same time torsional twisting of the long chassis did have an effect on the body frame and very few have survived the forty years that have passed since they were built.

With similar tail treatment to the Le Mans Special the four seater Mark II on a 10' wheelbase chassis was a popular family model that sold quite well.

Expensive at £750 the Mark II saloon was a beautiful creation but suffered from being under powered.

A piece of machinery

THE 100 MPH ULSTER

'A piece of machinery' is how H.S. Lindfield described the
Bertelli brothers' joint masterpiece. It embodied all their vast
experience of building cars for long distance racing and it was
in such events that it excelled. Being inherently heavy it was less
of an all rounder than its immediate competitors, the lighter and
more accelerative Rileys, MGs and Frazer-Nash, but because of
its massive construction it was immensely tough and that splendid
dry sump engine ensured such durability that almost all of the
seventeen laid down are still in existence and in many cases still
racing in vintage sports car events. In its day it was seen in action
at Ulster, Brooklands, Le Mans, Donnington Park, in the Mille
Miglia, the Targo Abruzzo and the Belgian and South African
Grand Prix where drivers of the calibre of 'Bira', Clarke, Falkner,
Donkin, Hamilton, Strazza and Count Lurani considered it worthy
of their skill.

In appearance the *Ulster* was faultless, the narrow doorless body
being a replica of the 1934 team cars with flat scuttle and spare
wheel laid flat in the base of the tail. The chassis was basically
that of the *Mark II*, assembled, tuned and split pinned to works'
specification. The engine with special Laystall fully balanced
crankshaft developed 80 bhp at 5250 rpm. Each car was guaranteed
to exceed 100 mph.

Priced at £750 the *Ulster* was indeed a unique motor car, a 'piece
of machinery' upholding the manufacturers' claim of being sold
ready to race without any further preparation.

The NEW "ULSTER" Model ASTON-MARTIN

● Guaranteed
Maximum Speed
100 M.P.H

● A Replica of the three cars which ran so successfully in the 1934 T.T. Race, finishing 3rd, 8th and 7th, and winning the TEAM PRIZE

● Also making a new lap record at 77.4 m.p.h. in Class F.

To own one of these "ULSTER" Model Aston-Martins is to experience "the real thing" in road racing, and to achieve higher average speeds and more consistent successes than ever before.

Moreover, they are built for durability with such precision that they hold their tune and maintain their performance with remarkable regularity.

SPECIFICATION
of the ASTON - MARTIN "ULSTER" MODEL

ENGINE 4-cyl. 69 m.m. bore x 99 m.m. stroke, 1495 cc., R.A.C. rating 11.9 h.p.   Max. B.H.P. 80 at 5250 r.p.m.   Compression Ratio 9.5/1.

This engine is specially finished and balanced and is capable of 5500 r.p.m. with safety. It is fitted with two large carburetters, special valves and valve springs, and has all inlet and exhaust passages highly polished.

GEAR RATIOS   The standard gear ratios are:—

Top 4.11	giving 102	m.p.h.
3rd 5.22	„ 80.75	m.p.h.
2nd 7.15	„ 50.0	m.p.h.
1st 11.5	„ 36.25	m.p.h.

at 5000 r.p.m. with 18 x 5.25 wheels and tyres.

Special ratios can be supplied at extra cost.

FUEL SUPPLY   The tank, holding 15 gallons, is carried immediately behind the drivers seat, and is fitted with two fillers.   Two electric pumps.   Reserve two gallons.

EQUIPMENT   Five R.W. wheels, 18 x 5.25 tyres, 4in. Rev. Counter, 4in. clock, oil pressure gauge, water thermometer, oil thermometer, ammeter, twin electric horns, lamp stone guards.   All switches fitted on instrument board.   Long ignition lever in centre of steering column.

BODY   2-Seater built specially light and panelled in Aluminium to A.I.A.C.R. Regulations.

Safety glass windscreen, fitted with side panels which can be used as small wind shields when screen is lowered.

Hood to fold inside body.

Spare wheel carried in tail of car in a flat position.

Price Complete as above £750

ASTON-MARTIN LIMITED   **FELTHAM, MIDDLESEX**

Phone: Feltham 218

The legendary Ulster was the Bertelli brothers' masterpiece and was never portrayed more beautifully than in the official Motor Show hand-out.

Daddy knows best

SUPERCHARGED ULSTERS

With its guaranteed speed of 100 mph the standard *Ulster* had the distinction of being the fastest production Aston Martin up to that time and so it is not surprising that one or two enthusiasts should be misled into thinking that the addition of a supercharger would provide them with the fastest Aston of them all. A smart piece of one-upmanship but had they sought advice from the works, they would have been told not to waste their money, for Bertelli knew from costly experience that the 1½ litre A.M. engine was strangely adverse to having its charge forcibly inducted.

However, at least two *Ulsters* (one an ex-works' car) were experimented with in this manner, the most successful being the creation of Messrs M.A. McEvoy of Derby, who held the British patent rights to the Zoller vane type supercharger. In their adaptation carried out to the order of amateur racing driver Flt. Lt. J.D. Greaves, the blower was fitted high on the offside alongside the rocker cover, the drive being taken from the timing gears at the front of the power unit. Whilst the young RAF officer competed with the car at both Brooklands and Donnington, it certainly failed to set the Thames on fire and the blower was later discarded.

The second contender for the honour of being the fastest *Ulster* remains something of a mystery. It was illustrated in *The Autocar* with an evasive caption and was never referred to again. Close examination of the original photograph suggests that this was a new, unregistered car stripped for racing. The blower (a Roots or Marshall component?) appears to have been driven directly off the nose of the crankshaft, being mounted between the dumb irons with the radiator suitably modified. The engineer responsible is unknown but it has been suggested that it could have been R.F. Oates the OM specialist.

The Zoller compressor as applied to an Ulster cylinder head by the late Laurence Pomeroy jnr, who was consultant to M.A. McEvoy, holder of the British patent rights.

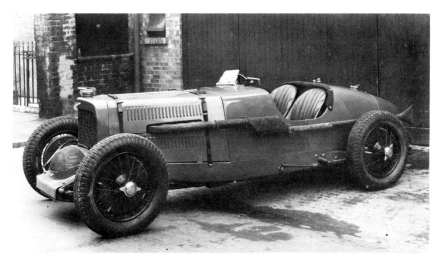

Presenting something of a mystery to Aston Martin historians is this Ulster with Roots type supercharger mounted between the front dumb irons.

Of limited appeal
THE MARK II DROPHEAD COUPE

No sooner had the *Mark II* long chassis been put into production than L. Prideaux-Brune, the London distributor, ordered a special drophead coupe version for his personal use in rallies, one of the many forms of competition in which he and his works' manager, the late C.M. Anthony participated regularly. The resulting car, finished in dark blue, was very handsome with two doors, wider than on the saloon, wind-down windows and exterior hood irons. The tail with exposed spare wheel and the interior seating arrangements were similar to the saloon as was the extended bonnet first used by Harry Bertelli some years earlier on the special *International* coupé made for W. Headlam (see page 90). The outside exhaust and cycle wings were typical Aston Martin, but the buzzer giving audible warning when a speed of 30 mph was reached, was an unnecessary though topical gimmick in view of the recent introduction of a speed limit in urban areas. In his first outing with the new car, the 1935 *RAC Eastbourne Rally,* Prideaux-Brune won the first prize for coachwork in the £501 - £700 class, and in the *Welsh Rally* later in the year, repeated this performance.

Subsequently some half dozen replicas were built for sale by the Winter Garden Garage but the model was never featured in the manufacturers' catalogue although it was mentioned in the motoring press as being available at £710, a figure rather naughtily outside the limit of Prideaux-Brune's rally awards!

An elegant Mark II drophead coupé built for L. Prideaux-Brune seen here with bare headed Morris-Goodall on his left.

The Winter Garden Garages were the most active of agents both the Managing Director, L. Prideaux-Brune, and Service Manager, the late C.M. 'Dick' Anthony competing regularly in all manner of competitions.

The last of a line
THE 1935 WORKS' CARS

'The best cars I ever built', is how Bertelli describes the four cars assembled for the 1935 season which as things turned out were destined to be the last full works' team with which the brilliant designer-builder-driver was to be associated and rather sadly he did not drive that year, electing to act as team manager, a job which in previous years had been performed by Sammy Davis who following Kensington-Moir's earlier assignments had developed a pit organisation unrivalled since the golden days of the Bentleys.

The new cars were distinguishable from the 1934 cars by having shorter radiators and sloping bonnets on each side of which was emblazoned the makers' name thus revising a custom of the 1920's which one thought had been outlawed by the RAC who nevertheless accepted the cars thus ornamented for the *Tourist Trophy* race so perhaps their scrutineer was descended from Nelson! And, once again, the cars were painted Italian red.

The chassis, with undrilled frames, for both Le Mans and Ulster, were similar to the 1934 cars but with engines now developing 85 bhp at 5250 rpm, an increase of five horse power. Maximum speed was well in access of 105 mph.

Three cars, LM18, 19 and 20 ran at *Le Mans* together with four private entries. Of this formidable armada one works' car crashed and the others all finished in 3rd, 8th, 10th, 11th, 12th and 15th positions overall. The two Charles, Martin and Brackenbury, were highest placed and also won the *Rudge Cup*. The crashed car was re-built in time for the *TT* and the team augmented by a further car, LM21. They won the team award and finished 4th, 5th and

11th, the fourth car being flagged off at the finish.

Altogether a highly successful year for the marque and a fitting swan song for the 1½ litre Aston Martin whose last year of production this proved to be, although cars were still being sold ex-stock during 1936 whilst production of the new 2 litre was getting under way.

This particularly interesting photograph shows the 1935 works' team being prepared at Feltham for the Tourist Trophy.

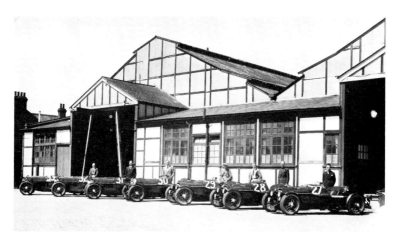

No less than seven Astons ran at Le Mans in 1935, three new works' cars with sloping bonnets seen on the right and four privately entered Ulsters distinguishable by their taller radiators.

J.C.C.
"DOUBLE 12"
BROOKLANDS

ANOTHER SUCCESS FOR
ASTON=MARTIN

In this great international race, contested by the world's
finest cars, the Aston-Martin achieved yet another success.

4th IN THE WHOLE RACE
2nd IN CLASS F
1770.28 miles at 73.76 m.p.h.

Let us demonstrate this wonderful British car. We are
Concessionnaires for London and the Southern Counties.

KENSINGTON-MOIR & STRAKER LTD.
23, GEORGE ST., HANOVER SQ.,
LONDON, W.1. *Phone:* MAYFAIR 1464-5. *Grams:* "SWIFTFLYT·WESDO·LONDON"

SERVICE:- 34, QUEEN'S GATE PLACE MEWS, SOUTH KENSINGTON. LONDON

Pride in achievement!

146

PART III

1936 - 1940

GORDON SUTHERLAND AND THE 2 LITRES

R. Gordon Sutherland who with Claude Hill was responsible for the development
of the 2 litre Aston Martin after the departure of A.C. Bertelli and made the
model a commercial success.

INTRODUCTION

In 1935 the Mark II Aston Martin 2/4 seater was catalogued at £610. Only two other 1½ litre cars on the British Market exceeded this figure. They were the unrealistically priced Squire at £995 and the exorbitantly priced twin-cam Frazer Nash listed at £625. For sums considerably less even than the Aston, indeed for well under £400, the sporting motorist had a wide choice of fast, well engineered motor cars. Not as exclusive perhaps as the Aston Martin but a £200 premium was a lot of money to spend on individuality. In the 1500 cc class there was the British Salmson with twin overhead camshaft at only £365, the Frazer Nash BMW, not yet fully acceptable to British eyes, but with a sparkling performance for only £335, the Riley, mass produced but with a magnificent engine costing £372, the Singer Le Mans, definitely a 'boys racer' yet with a contemporary competition background at £350 and cheapest of all at £315, the very nice Lea-Francis, albeit with a fading competition record. Even Geoffrey Taylor was able to offer his exciting if temperamental Alta for as little as £450! In the 2 litre class one could purchase for £495 a nicely built AC with an interesting well proven power unit, (good enough to be seriously considered by Sutherland and Bertelli as an alternative power unit for their Mark II saloon). And Alvis offered their near-mass produced 'Firebird' for just under £500.

These then were the facts of life facing the Aston Martin directorate, not forgetting Winter Garden Garage and the lesser distributors who between them found it impossible to dispose of the 100 Mark IIs laid down for 1935 within the twelve months. Its individuality, the fact that it was genuinely hand-made (although less so than the earlier models) and its highly successful racing pedigree still being maintained just could not justify that £200 margin over the selling price of its 1½ litre competitors. Obviously something had to be done to make the Aston more competitive within its price range and Sutherland and Bertelli decided that the answer was a more powerful engine. As a start, other manufacturers' power units were considered including the 2 litre AC, a specimen being in the works for some time and although highly thought of, not proceeded with. Then came the more exciting possibility of using the six cylinder 2300 twin over-head camshaft Alfa-Romeo but these plans did not materialise either although negotiations reached quite an advanced stage. Meanwhile Claude Hill sketched out several ideas including an 8 cylinder twin cam engine. Bertelli also showed considerable interest in the Cross Rotary Valve, a project later revised by Sutherland after Bertelli had left the firm.

Then someone recalled a special *International* coupé built some years earlier for W.S. Headlam who had had it bored out to 1750 cc quite transorming the car's performance with a top speed of nearly 100 mph. It was decided to conduct similar experiments with the Mark II which again resulted in a marked improvement in power output. Gordon Sutherland in one of his helpful letters to the author comments on the subsequent develop-ment in detail, 'When the 2 litre project got the go ahead, this development was continued and a 2 litre engine with same side porting as the 1½ litre was run on the bench. I do not know what prompted it but another head was then tried with opposite porting and gave definitely better results. This engine was fitted on BME 399 the original Mark II, which we kept as demonstrator. Bertelli ran this for a long time and it became known as the *Blue Car*. It would do over 90 mph and had very good acceleration ... better than my 4/4 litre Bentley. 'Dick' Anthony tried it and was very impressed. He persuaded Bertelli to let him do the same on one of Winter Garden's cars. The bore and stroke must have been 78 mm x 102 mm, the same as other 2 litres. The 1750 cc experimental engine had the 1½ litre stroke, 99 mm, so the bore must have been dangerously large for the block, nearly 80 mm. Perhaps they were less than 1750 cc ... 78 mm bore gives 1700 cc'.

Resulting from these series of experiments, Bertelli decided he could built a full 2 litre engine using the existing patterns and jigs with comparatively inexpensive modifications. This was obviously going to save a good deal of money and he and Claude Hill were on surer ground in developing the well tried 1½ litre.

The finalised design with bore and stroke of 78 mm x 102 mm, giving a total capacity of 1949 cc, was planned to be made in two forms, a touring engine with wet sump and the speed model with the traditional dry sump. It was anticipated that the new car, for the chassis too was new, in speed model form would prove a good deal more competitive than even the *Ulster* and two cars were entered for the 1936 *Le Mans* which was cancelled at very short notice due to political strife in France.

Sutherland doubts however if the Astons would have been very successful anyhow for due to the powerful Lockheed brakes much trouble was experienced with the cracking of drum liners. Under the Le Mans regulations 25 similar chassis had had to be built and after the cancellation of the race most of these were put to one side in order that the works could concentrate on the big programme of saloons and tourers planned for launching at the Motor Show in October. These touring models with a wheelbase of 9' 8" were much more commodious and practical than any previous A.M. and quite handsome in their way but in abolishing the familiar cycle wings a good deal of the car's individuality had gone. The Show opened and the new models, most competitively priced at £495 upwards, were well received, a number of orders being placed.

Unfortunately the cars had only just been completed and there had been no chance to drive them before the show when serious teething troubles would have been revealed. To quote Sutherland 'The first hint of trouble was when Bertelli was able to try the second saloon which had been put aside as demonstrator. He reported it as ... very rough and noisy ... by the New Year we realised that the saloons were going to be a real headache although the tourers were very good'. This was quite a serious

THE SPORTS CAR BECOMES LUXURIOUS

𝒴OU may know the Aston Martin as a Sports Car.

You are going to know the new Two-Litre as much more. To the

speed, the road-holding and reliability which has won fame on road and

race track, are now added the superlative comfort and effortless running

of the modern luxury car. Open Four-Seater £575. Saloon £595.

ASTON·MARTIN

FAST LUXURY

ASTON MARTIN LTD. FELTHAM MIDDLESEX.   PHONE: FELTHAM 2291.

An early advertisement of the 2 litre model.

Looking back and looking forward. Gordon Sutherland's classic war time advertisement.

crisis and Sutherland took the only action that seemed possible, reduce the number of saloons and transfer to open coachwork more suitable for the rough 2 litre engine. This roughness seems inherent in 'big fours' and was experienced years later by Walter Hassan when developing the four cylinder XK engine for Jaguar, which was not proceeded with for this very reason. And so the order with E. Bertelli Ltd for 100 saloon bodies for the Aston was halved and immediate production concentrated on the tourer which after a good deal of work by Claude Hill was good value for money and not nearly such a bad car as many would make it out to be. Sutherland never intended it to be an Aston Martin in the old tradition and Bertelli now thoroughly disheartened by the way things were going sadly resigned from the company.

The cars also suffered from front axle tramp due to the more flexible springing and wider track than the smaller cars. This was overcome by fitting Wilmot Breedon 'Harmonic' stabilising bumpers which Sutherland always considered a compromise and led to experiments with a semi-space frame body.

The problem with the brake drums splitting on the *Speed Models* was more difficult to cure. They had to be modified several times eventually finishing up with light alloy cooling fins shrunk on.

However, by the summer of 1937 most of the problems had been sorted out, at least with the tourers and the following October a short chassis with 8' 6" wheelbase was made available with a close coupled 2/4 seater body and a drophead coupe. Both were powered by the wet sump engine.

To the die hard enthusiast these Astons, although sporting might have lost a good deal of the marque's earlier appeal but the new range of models undoubtedly attracted a much wider market than hitherto and Sutherland's policy seemed to be successful. But he was still something of an enthusiast and was anxious to augment the range with a sports model more in line with the car's earlier prestige. Current trends, as exemplified by the 328 BMW, indicated that the traditional *Ulster* style of sports car was obsolete and in order to test public reaction one of the 'cocooned' *Speed Model* chassis was fitted with a streamlined sports body of tear drop shape and exhibited at the 1938 show. Its introduction coincided with a praiseworthy 2nd place in the *TT* at Donnington Park by St. John Horsfall on his own *Ulster* bodied *Speed Model*. The resultant publicity drew considerable attention to the *C* type as the new streamlined model was designated, but public and press reaction was only luke warm for it was neither fish nor fowl, the advanced body styling concealing a somewhat outdated cart sprung chassis with beam axles and powered by an engine dating back to the mid-twenties. Nevertheless the half dozen remaining *Speed Model* chassis were dusted off, fitted with the re-designed brake drums and mounted with *C* type bodies differing slightly from the prototype.

Behind the scenes much more exciting things were on Claude Hill's drawing board. With sales of the cheaper 2 litres maintaining a satisfactory level Sutherland was able to give his designer a free hand in preparing an entirely new Aston Martin intended to match anything forthcoming from rival firms here or on the Continent. Claude Hill grasped this opportunity with boldness and imagination, quick to appreciate the changing requirements of the time and prepared to abandon traditional features of design and manufacture.

The outcome of this new thinking was the *Atom* with body and chassis built in one unit with independent front suspension, Cotal gearbox and, in the final stages of development, a completely new push rod engine.

Plans for production were hindered by the outbreak of war which at the same time extended opportunities for thorough testing and the car covered more than 100,000 miles during the period of hostilities.

In embryo the *Atom* was a magnificent motor car which with the changing conditions of peace was beyond the capacity of the company to manufacture in the quantities it deserved. The design was sold together with name, assets and what-have-you to industrialist David Brown. A new chapter in Aston Martin history was about to begin.

For a while Claude Hill remained with the firm which moved to other premises a short distance away from the historic works which had suffered in the blitz, before joining Ferguson Research where he is still very active.

Gordon Sutherland continued to service the older Astons from Friary Motors at Old Windsor and also took over the coachbuilding firm of Abbotts at Farnham. Today he lives in retirement in Ireland, his contribution to the survival of the Aston Martin car sadly neglected by motoring historians.

TO   THE   WEST   COUNTRY   FOR   LUNCH

Always fast - but never flurried!

ONLY after arrival do you realise the speed at which you came····. in this silent and luxurious "15/98" Aston Martin. For out of a brilliant racing tradition has been created a new entity. With a silky-smooth engine developing its power so sweetly, the luxury of this car irresistibly reminds you of a limousine .... that is capable of well over 80 m.p.h. Open Four-Seater £575. Saloon £595. Olympia Stand No. 83

NEW "15/98" h.p.

ASTON MARTIN

fast luxury

ASTON MARTIN LTD. FELTHAM, MIDDLESEX.   PHONE: FELTHAM 2291.

Keymer

A false start

THE 2 LITRE WORKS' CARS OF 1936

In the summer of 1936 France was embroiled in a wave of industrial strikes and L'Automobile Club de L'Ouest were compelled to abandon their classic 24 hours race at Le Mans. Notice of the cancellation was announced only at the very last moment which was a severe blow to manufacturers and entrants of no less than 60 cars many of them prepared specially for this one event.

For Aston Martins it was a particularly severe setback for the first of their new 2 litre cars had been completed and they were hoping to make a successful debut on the Sarthe circuit, but with hindsight Gordon Sutherland doubts that they would have done very well as the cars were very much in prototype form and there were development problems with brakes and front suspension. The two cars prepared for Le Mans presented a curious blend of *Ulster* style traditionalism and half hearted acknowledgement of the new streamline approach being pioneered on the Continent. Lockheed hydraulic brakes were the most progressive item in what was otherwise very much a conventional, though wider, Aston chassis with semi-elliptic suspension damped by Hartford shock absorbers.

The new 1949 cc engine of 78 mm x 102 mm bore and stroke was very similar to the smaller cars using the patented R & B cylinder head but with the ports reversed left to right. A Scintilla Vertex magneto was a modern innovation and dry sump lubrication was retained.

Following the cancellation of Le Mans the two cars were sold, one to C.H. Woods the works' service manager and the other to J.C. Elwes a director of the Cresta Motor Company of Worthing who were area distributors for Aston Martin. With co-driver Sir Alistair MacRobert, Elwes competed in the *Belgian 24 Hours Race* at Spa where the car ran well until being put out with a split fuel tank. As consolation they were awarded the Jacques de Liedekerke Trophy for the most meritorious performance put up by a non-finisher.

The first 2 litre. One of a pair built for the cancelled Le Mans race of 1936. The car under construction in the left background is one of the Graham British Specials produced in small numbers by E. Bertelli Ltd.

A nearside view of the team car's dry sump engine showing its basic similarity to the earlier 1½ litre, more obvious differences being the transposed ports and Scintilla 'Vertex' magneto.

A brilliant failure
THE SEAMAN AND PHIPPS 2 LITRE RACERS

Following the splendid showing of the new 2 litre at Spa, two further racing cars were prepared for clients. The first of these went to A.R. Phipps, an American enthusiast who was resident in this country and married Doreen Evans whose family were well known MG exponents. Richard Seaman whom many considered to be the greatest British driver at that time, took delivery of the second car which he entered for the *RAC Tourist Trophy*, as did Phipps.

Both cars were near replicas of the ex-works cars prepared for *Le Mans* but with revised wing treatments and minor body differences. In order to obviate any problems with the fuel tanks as experienced at Spa, the frames were suitably strengthened at the rear. Seaman was given extensive support by the works who were well aware of the potential value success in the *TT* would bring in the hands of such a driver. But it was not to be! In heavy rain the Britisher put up a magnificent performance in his black car taking the class record at 75.89 mph ahead of the works' team of BMWs. Then the bearings gave out on his engine which had been hastily re-assembled on the very eve of the race following similar trouble during practise.

Phipps, not a very experienced driver, ran off the road and his car was badly damaged. Seaman's drive impressed everyone and following the 2 litre's promising maiden run at Spa it seemed all the more regrettable when the factory decided to withdraw from the racing scene due to 'the prevailing economic climate'.

The ex-Seaman car was sold to a Continental driver but after the war was brought back to this country where John Wyer and Dudley Folland re-built it as 'Red Dragon' under which name it proceeded to establish a phenomenal record in vintage events of all kinds.

Better streamlined wings distinguished the two racers built for Richard Seaman and A.R. Phipps from the works' cars. This is Phipps' car during tests at Brooklands.

This front view shows the rather cumbersome cowling and Lockheed brakes.

Less sporting, less costly
THE 15/98 CHASSIS

Gordon Sutherland was not only an enthusiast but also a very capable business man and the economic conditions of the time convinced him that 'due to the high figure at which our class of work must always be priced, it was essential that a sports saloon become our main model even to the exclusion of open sports models if this was unavoidable, otherwise the model was too limited to enable the firm to carry on'. A realistic decision which inevitably met with cries of anguish from a great many enthusiasts who in most cases were far from being prospective customers, a situation still existing today in a much more affluent age.

The new model, known as the *15/98*, used basically the same frame as the 2 litre prototypes extended to 9' 8" wheelbase with Girling brakes in place of the Lockheeds and Luvax shock absorbers at the rear and Hartfords retained at the front. A major departure from traditional A.M. practise was the abandonment of the famous dry sump lubrication system which, splendid as it was, had probably always met with a certain amount of sales resistance. The gearbox was of Moss manufacture with synchromesh on the three upper ratios.

By using a larger proportion of bought out parts than hitherto, combined with a planned production of 150 cars, it was possible without departing from A.M.'s high standard of workmanship, to offer a stripped chassis at £498, some £200 less than the dry sump sports chassis now listed as the *Speed Model* of which no further examples were assembled beyond the original twenty-five.

Works' records would appear to have lacked any photos of the 15/98 chassis in stripped form but thanks to AMOC member Peter Engelbach, it is possible to illustrate his concours winning model taken during restoration. It is completely original save for the fabricated alloy bulkhead.

Transformation

THE 15/98 SALOON AND TOURER

'The sports car becomes luxurious' proclaimed Aston Martin advertising at the time of the 1936 Olympia Show when their new *15/98* models made their debut. In truth a transformation had taken place but whether in fact the new saloon was more luxurious than the smaller Mark II is debateable. It was certainly more spacious but equally less sporting although good value for money at £595 for the saloon and £575 for the tourer, E. Bertelli being responsible for the coachwork.

Both models were well received by the press and, more important-ly, by a very much wider buying public than had previously shown any interest in the marque. The saloon bore a passing resemblance to the lovely Mark II saloon but lacked the smaller car's low sleek lines. The high sided tourer was a full four seater with swept wings and vestigal running boards duplicated on the closed model. Equipment was comprehensive and included Smiths' inbuilt 'Jackall' hydraulic jacks, a real luxury in those days when punctures were far more common than they are today. They were also a practical feature for the owner who carried out his own servicing. Several orders were taken in the first two days of the Show and things looked very bright indeed until Bertelli came to run the saloon demonstrator for the first time. He reported it as being rough and noisy with the anticipated luxurious performance sadly lacking. Various modifications were quickly explored which led to the fitting of Wilmot-Breedon harmonic stabilising bumpers. Other less visible changes were made which helped improve matters and deliveries commenced early in 1937.

In June 1938 prices were reduced by no less than £100 on each model which made them very competitive indeed and they continued in production with little further change up to the outbreak of war.

Original sketches suggested the 15/98 saloon might have born a closer resemblance to the beautiful Mark II saloon than it actually did, but when eventually produced it looked too much like the contemporary SS and Triumphs to be really outstanding.

The Aston Martin 15/98 Open Four Seater

Oct: 1937

The large single door on each side of the 15/98 open four seater rather emphasized its length and detracted from its appearance.

Personal choice

A VINTAGE 2 SEATER AND THE FASTEST CAR PRE-WAR

When at the 1936 Motor Show, the wet sump *15/98* model was introduced the remaining twenty or so dry sump chassis laid down under the Le Mans regulations were catalogued as the *Speed Model* and offered in chassis form only at £695 but there were only two buyers. The first was the late W.G. Barlow, a personal friend of the Bertellis whose allegiance to the marque dated back to the old Lionel Martin days.

Barlow's car with an exposed rear tank and cycle pattern wings was quite vintage in appearance and although built by Harry Bertelli was probably based on the client's own sketches for in addition to being a skilled model maker he was a prolific freelance 'designer' of bodies based on Aston Martin chassis. The second special was ordered by R.S. Wilkins and fitted with an *Ulster* body which was 'found' discarded in a corner of the 'end shop'. After one or two appearances at Brooklands the car passed into the hands of St. John Horsfall, a young enthusiast who had gained a lot of experience racing an *International*. He set about re-assembling, modifying and tuning the two litre until eventually it achieved the distinction of being the fastest Aston Martin of pre-war days, living proof that old fashioned though it might have been Bertelli's two litre had a tremendous potential never fully exploited by the works. Stripped of wings, the Horsfall car lapped Brooklands' outer circuit at over 108 mph, its maximum speed being little short of 120 mph.

With more than ample ground clearance the special vintage style Speed Model built for R.G. Barlow was not a particularly successful exercise.

St. John Horsfall's remarkably successful 2 litre Speed Model with Ulster body grafted on is seen here at Brooklands. Comedian Geroge Formby is seated beside the owner/driver while Mrs Beryl Formby poses on the tail.

Sports cars again
SPEED MODEL VARIANTS BY TWO COACHBUILDERS

Having managed to sell only two *Speed Model* chassis, an effort was made to dispose of some of the remaining nineteen examples by having E. Bertelli complete seven with 2/4 seater bodies and Abbey Coachworks of Willesden a pair of 2 seaters. The latter, which were never catalogued, were very sporting in the vintage style with rounded tails and fixed cycle wings. They were sold directly from the works to a Mr Stopford who also had a 2/4 seater and to N. Bond-Williams who drove his with some success in minor events at Brooklands and Donnington Park.

The Bertelli 2/4 seater versions were quite nice looking cars but very different from the traditional sports Astons having tall inclined radiator shells, long sweeping wings and short sloping tails. Their performance however was dismal and not comparable with the *Ulster*. In plan view they were almost square and although developing 105/110 bhp this was absorbed in overcoming the increased weight and wind resistance. By fitting special low axle ratios they eventually were made to exceed 90 mph but the high cost of hand cutting the gears together with the modified brake drums fitted to all the *Speed Models* (at a cost of £20 each drum!) could hardly have made these cars a commercial proposition.

The remaining chassis were put under dust sheets where they remained for two years until being fitted with streamlined *C*-type bodies which were slow to sell, the last car being disposed of some eighteen months after the outbreak of war by which time car production generally had well and truly ceased and any new car was at a premium.

The Aston Martin 15/98 Speed Model

Harry Bertelli's version of the Speed Model although having pleasing lines was too heavy and poorly streamlined thus failing to exploit the full potential of its chassis.

More vintage in appearance was the Abbey bodied 2 seater but this was not the answer either and only a pair were built.

Development and experiment

THE DONALD DUCK SALOON AND ROTARY VALVES

A.C. Bertelli's departure from Feltham early in 1937 left R. Gordon Sutherland in complete managerial control and assisted by Claude Hill who loyally stayed with the firm, he was faced with two unenviable tasks; to iron out the bugs in the 2 litre, both the *15/98* and the *Speed Model*, and to keep the firm in business during a very difficult economic period.

First step was to commandeer the Show saloon which during the next three years was to serve as works' guinea pig. Step by step countless developments and experiments were adapted on this car, some to be incorporated in the production models and others discarded, but sometimes filed for future use.

A major development which was to have a far reaching effect in the history of the Aston Martin car was the construction of a new steel panelled body built up around a box section frame fabricated from electrical conduit, a material readily and economically available during a period of extensive arms production which had first call on better quality material. The method of construction used in the prototype saloon limited the body contours resulting in an oddly shaped saloon with a high roof line. Known in the factory as *Donald Duck*, it was, says Sutherland, 'most successful and very pleasant to drive. If only the original 2 litre had been half as good, Astons' commercial future would have been assured, but it was a year too late.' Further evidence of the company's new found taste for adventure was an unsuccessful flirtation with the cross rotary valve, cleverly adapted by Claude Hill to a *Speed Model* block. This proved highly temperamental, taking two days to start at the first attempt. With the valve providing a good seal, friction was too high and when the seal was eased there was no compression, and even with the co-operation of its designer, that most likeable person Mr R.C. Cross, Sutherland failed to make it a viable proposition.

Nicknamed 'Donald Duck' this oddly shaped saloon body concealed many advanced features of design which through the C-type and the Atom led directly to the post war DB 1 and DB 2.

Illustrative of Gordon Sutherland's willingness to experiment was designer Claude Hill's clever adaptation of the Cross Rotary Valve to a Speed Model cylinder block. Unfortunately in practise it failed to consolidate the theoretical advantages and was eventually scrapped.

TWO SPECIAL COMPETITION CARS

Lance Prideaux-Brune who for so many years had acted as London distributor for Aston Martin, demonstrated his faith in the new 2 litre by renewing his concession and at the same time ordering a special drophead coupé for his own use in rallies and concours d'elegance. Built by E. Bertelli Ltd, it followed earlier cars of this style that Prideaux-Brune had owned and rallied, but was not nearly as handsome as these special bodies in the 1½ litre class.

Mounted on the long chassis this new coupe was hump-backed with somewhat shapeless rear quarter windows. Despite winning a coachwork award in the 1937 *RAC Rally*, it failed to receive much acclaim from A.M. enthusiasts and no replicas were built as had been the case with the earlier Mark II coupé.

Another special of a vastly different kind was not really a special at all but a development of the ex-Seaman TT car and is included here to illustrate the efforts made by several people to extract the full potential of the 2 litre *Speed Model*. In this case the re-modelling and slimming down of the front end was the work of the German driver E. Hertzberger who raced the car, now painted orange, in the 1937 *Mille Miglia* coming second in his class. At *Le Mans* in the same year he retired after leading the Hitchens-Morris-Goodall 2 litre for several hours. The latter car (the ex-Elwes works' car) eventually finished in 11th place, another example of how keen amateurs were able to develop the *Speed Model* into extremely worthwhile competition cars.

The Hertzberger car was brought back to England after the war and further developed by Dudley Folland who re-named it *Red Dragon* and in that form is still very active in vintage events.

Probably the least attractive of Prideaux-Brune's special bodied Astons was his 2 litre coupe built for the 1937 RAC Rally.

It was rare for pre-war Astons to be owned and raced by Continental drivers, but after re-styling the front end of his ex-Seaman Speed Model, E. Hertzberger was active on the Continent including appearances at Le Mans and in the 1937 Mille Miglia.

A short chassis once more

THE 15/98 COUPE AND 2/4 SEATER

New for the 1937 London Show, the first to be held at Earls Court, was an 8' 3" wheelbase chassis with the wet sump engine. The dry sump *Speed Model* was still catalogued but there were no takers.

Two standard body styles were made available on the new short chassis, a sporting 2/4 seater and a drophead coupé. The open model had quite attractive lines but at 24 cwt it was a relatively heavy car and the performance suffered accordingly, a maximum of 82 mph being recorded by *The Autocar*, no better indeed than the old 1½ litre. It was listed at £575. The coupé cost an additional £50 and was quite an elegant motor car but as usual with its type, suffered from blind rear quarters. The hood was easily managed and there were wind-up windows in the doors. The outside dickey seat was not very easy to get out of, even though steps were provided on the near side wing. Altogether 25 were built by Abbotts of Farnham, Abbey Coachworks were responsible for 50 2/4 seaters. E. Bertelli Ltd in fulfilling their curtailed contract continued to build the long chassis saloons and tourers, 25 of the former and 50 of the latter.

Although Winter Garden Garage announced their re-appointment as London distributors at the time of the Show, by the following March the manufacturers had assumed responsibility for all sales and had opened a service department at Feltham which was personally supervised by Gordon Sutherland and of which he was particularly proud.

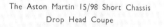

The Aston Martin 15/98 Short Chassis
Drop Head Coupe

One of the better looking 2 litres was the drophead coupe on the short 15/98 chassis introduced in 1937.

Also on the short chassis was the 2/4 seater the most sporting of the 'bread and butter' 2 litres.

A curious blend of ancient and modern
THE C-TYPE 2 SEATER

Increased production of the *15/98* models brought about by a reduction in price combined with a vigorous sales policy placed the works in the happy position of working to capacity and thus precluded any thought of re-entry into the International racing scene, at least for the time being, but Sutherland had not lost his interest in true high performance cars and gave amateur driver St. John Horsfall considerable works assistance in preparing his *Ulster* bodied *Speed Model* which came second in the *TT* at Donnington Park.

Experience gained in this exercise helped in ironing out various problems with the dry sump chassis of which quite a number remained at the works unsold. One of these was then up dated and fitted with a body of tear drop shape designed by Claude Hill and built within the works. Designated the *C* type, this was something of a compromise, a conventional yet potent chassis clothed in a 'modern' body framed in square sectioned steel tubing. With hindsight it provided a broad hint as to the way the wind was blowing down Feltham way, confirming, following the building of *Donald Duck*, that Claude Hill had advanced ideas which Sutherland was prepared to back to the full extent of the available financial resources.

The first *C* type was exhibited at Earls Court in 1938 and attracted considerable if controversial attention. On the show model the lamps were mounted on the wings each side of a shield shaped radiator grill that sloped to the front dumb irons, access to the oil tank filler being through a hinged flap in the front fairing. Subsequent examples, of which seven were built on the remaining

Speed Model chassis, had the lamps behind the radiator grill, which was of a different shape, the whole frontal appearance anticipating the 'C' type Jaguar by thirteen years. These streamlined Astons were genuine 100 mph cars and in fact Sutherland attained 112 mph at Brooklands using oversize tyres and enclosed passenger seat.

In an effort to utilise the remaining small stock of Speed Model chassis the streamlined C-type 2 seater was exhibited at Earls Court in 1938.

Subsequent C-types (6 in all) had a revised frontal treatment which bore a remarkable resemblance to the C-type Jaguars of thirteen years later.

Single seaters

THE WORKS' MONOPOSTO AND THE FASTEST
PRE-WAR ASTON

Not since *Razor Blade* had there been such a special one-off
Aston Martin as the single seater concocted by Hill and Sutherland
for an attempt on the Brooklands 2 litre outer circuit record.
With its narrow rear track, angled steering column providing a
central driving position and fared head rest, it was a genuine
Brooklands car in the old tradition, not particularly aesthetic in
appearance yet purposeful in a brutal sort of way. It was originally
intended to use the Cross rotary valve engine in the car but the
war broke out before car or engine could be fully tested and, with
a normal Speed Model engine, it was put away for the duration.
After the David Brown take over of Aston Martins in 1947, the car
was purchased by Knaresborough coachbuilder Gordon Gartside
who converted it into a sports two seater, so we shall never know
its full potential.

Completely different in conception and execution was a second
single seater built by St. John Horsfall using as a basis a standard
2/4 seater Speed Model. This transformation took place in 1948
which strictly speaking is outside the period covered by this book,
but the car demands inclusion as it was the fastest pre-war Aston
ever built.

Using a good deal more scientific approach than did the works in
their single seater exercise and being in a position to discount
the hundreds of man hours devoted to his project, Horsfall was
able to achieve a speed of 140 mph using four Amal carburettors
and dope fuel. Brake horse power was quoted as being no less than
125. The driver-builder ran his car only once in single seater form,
at Luton Hoo, before adding road equipment and driving single
handed for 24 hours at Spa to gain second place in his class.

The outbreak of war unfortunately curtailed development of the works' single seater built for an attempt on the Brooklands outer circuit record.

Fastest of all pre-war Aston Martins (as distinct from Aston Martins pre-war) was the single seater built up by the late St. John Horsfall for the 1948 Formula B specification in which form it had an estimated top speed of 140 mph.

The new order of motoring

THE ATOM SALOON

The *Atom*, barely completed by the outbreak of war, was the prototype of a new generation of Aston Martins which might conceivably have been the stars of the show at Earls Court in 1940 had such an event taken place. As it was the war years provided an extended opportunity to test the car to a high pitch of perfection. Over 100,000 miles were covered in the course of which three engines were used, the final one being an entirely new overhead valve push rod design which was inherited by David Brown when he acquired the firm in 1947, and used by him in his first production model, the DB1.

In designing the *Atom*, Claude Hill set out to produce a car of advanced design that would be reasonably economical to build and would sell at a price comparable with the existing 2 litres. As we have seen, Feltham had accumulated considerable experience of steel framed body structures both with the *C* type 2 seater and, more particularly, the experimental saloon *Donald Duck*, but in planning the new car the designer went a stage further with a body and chassis made up of rectangular steel tubing varying in section according to the stresses imposed. The basic chassis frame itself possessed little torsional strength, but when welded in unit with the body frame produced a very rigid angular cage to which shaped formers were attached to provide the desired body contours which of course could be altered as fashion dictated. A further innovation which benefited from the still frame structure was the employment of Gordon Armstrong cantilever independent suspension at the front. Rear suspension was by long semi-elliptic springs.

Mechanical elements comprised a standard wet sump 2 litre engine with single plate Roper & Wreakes clutch driving via a Cotal electro magnetic pre-selector gearbox to a Salisbury hyphoid bevel rear axle which was a 'sample' introducing the American component to this country.

All in all a bold imaginative recipe best summed up by the late Laurence Pomeroy who writing in *The Motor* said 'we can see the new order of motoring before our very eyes'.

The prototype Atom saloon built around a skeleton frame and with independent front suspension was the last pre-war Aston Martin and indicative of the progressive ideas of Gordon Sutherland and Claude Hill. Built during a period of intensive Government re-armament policy its actual shape was dictated to some extent by the availability of materials.

APPENDIX I

TECHNICAL SPECIFICATIONS

TECHNICAL SPECIFICATIONS OF LIONEL MARTIN

PRODUCTION MODELS 1923 - 1925

	Touring Model	Sports Model	Super-Sports Model	Sports Model
Approx. production or catalogue period	1923 - 1925	1923 - 1925	1923 - 1925	1925
Number of cylinders	4	4	4	4
Bore & stroke	66.5 x 107 mm	66.5 x 107 mm	65 m 112 mm	65 x 112 mm
Capacity	1486 cc	1486 cc	1487 cc	1487 cc
Lubrication system	wet sump, pressure	wet sump, pressure	wet sump, pressure	wet sump, pressure
Valve location	side	side	16 valves, overhead	8 valves, overhead
Camshaft	in crankcase	in crankcase	twin overhead	twin overhead
Advertised power output			55 bhp at 4200 rpm	64 bhp at 4500 rpm
Clutch	Hele-Shaw	Hele-Shaw	Hele-Shaw	Hele-Shaw
Gearbox	separate 4-speed	separate 4-speed	separate 4-speed	separate 4-speed
Final drive	Bevel drive	Bevel drive	Bevel drive	Bevel drive
Brakes	4 wheel rod & cable operation	4 wheel rod & cable operation	4 wheel rod & cable operation	4 wheel rod & cable operation
Suspension	semi-elliptic	semi-elliptic	semi-elliptic	semi-elliptic
Chassis frame	upswept front & rear	upswept front & rear	upswept front & rear	upswept front & rear
Wheelbase	8' 9"	8' 0"	8' 0"	8' 9"
Track	4' 3"	4' 3"	4' 3"	4' 3"
Catalogued coachwork	no standard coachwork, but various designs listed	no standard coachwork, but various designs listed	2 seater	only 1 car built and exhibited at 1925 Olympia Show

TECHNICAL SPECIFICATIONS OF BERTELLI 1.5 LITRE PRODUCTION MODELS 1927 - 1936

	T - Type	Sports	International Sports	International Long Chassis
Approx. production or catalogue period	1927 - 1929	1927 - 1928 prototypes only	1929 - 1932	1930 - 1932
Number of cylinders	4	4	4	4
Bore & stroke	69 x 99 mm	69 x 99 mm	69 x 99 mm	69 x 99 mm
Capacity	1488 cc	1488 cc	1488 cc	1488 cc
Lubrication system	wet sump	wet & dry sump	dry sump	dry sump
Valve location	overhead	overhead	overhead	overhead
Camshaft	single overhead	single overhead	single overhead	single overhead
Advertised power output	-	-	56 bhp at 5500 rpm 63 bhp at 4750 rpm (Ulster engine)	-
Clutch	Borg & Beck	Borg & Beck	Borg & Beck	Borg & Beck
Gearbox	separate 4-speed	separate 4-speed	separate 4-speed	separate 4-speed
Final drive	worm	worm	worm	worm
Brakes	4 wheel rod & cable operated	4 wheel rod operated	4 wheel rod operated	4 wheel rod operated
Suspension	semi-elliptic	semi-elliptic	semi-elliptic	semi-elliptic
Chassis frame	upswept front & rear	underslung at rear	underslung at rear	underslung at rear
Wheelbase	9' 6" (1927 - 28) 9' 10" (1929)	?	8' 6"	9' 10"
Track	4' 4"	4' 4"	4' 4"	4' 4"
Catalogued coachwork	4 door saloon 4 seater tourer	3 seater	2 x 3 seater (1929) 2 or 2/4 seater (1930 - 31) drophead coupe (1931) Le Mans 2 seater sports (1931)	2 door sportsman's coupe (1930 - 31) 4 seater tourer (1931 - 31) 4 door saloon (1931 - 31) 2 door saloon (1931 - 32)

TECHNICAL SPECIFICATIONS OF BERTELLI 1.5 LITRE

PRODUCTION MODELS 1927 - 1936

	New International	12/50 Standard	Le Mans
Approx. production or catalogue period	1932	1932 - 1934	1932 - 1934
Number of cylinders	4	4	4
Bore & stroke	69 x 99 mm	69 x 99 mm	69 x 99 mm
Capacity	1488 cc	1488 cc	1488 cc
Lubrication system	dry sump	dry sump	dry sump
Valve location	overhead	overhead	overhead
Camshaft	single overhead	single overhead	single overhead
Advertised power output		55 bhp at 4500 rpm	70 bhp at 4750 rpm
Clutch	Borg & Beck	Borg & Beck	Borg & Beck
Gearbox	unit 4-speed	unit 4-speed	unit 4-speed
Final drive	spiral bevel	spiral bevel	spiral bevel
Brakes	4 wheel cable operated	4 wheel cable operated	4 wheel cable operated
Suspension	semi-elliptic underslung at rear	semi-elliptic underslung at rear	semi-elliptic underslung at rear
Chassis frame			
Wheelbase	8' 6"	10' 0"	8' 6"
Track	4' 4"	4' 4"	4' 4"
Catalogued coachwork	2/4 seater (1932) 2 seater Le Mans (sometimes known as competition 2 seater) (1932)	4 door saloon (1932 - 34) 4 seater tourer (1932 - 34)	2/4 seater (1932 - 34)

Le Mans Special	Mark II	Ulster
1933 - 1934	1934 - 1936	1934 - 1936
4	4	4
69 x 99 mm	69 x 99 mm	69 x 99 mm
1488 cc	1488 cc	1488 cc
dry sump	dry sump	dry sump
overhead	overhead	overhead
single overhead	single overhead	single overhead
70 bhp at 4750 rpm	73 bhp at 5200 rpm	80 bhp at 5250 rpm
	Borg & Beck	Borg & Beck
Borg & Beck	unit 4-speed	unit 4-speed
unit 4-speed	spiral bevel	spiral bevel
spiral bevel	4 wheel cable operated	4 wheel cable operated ′
4 wheel cable operated	semi-elliptic	semi-elliptic
semi-elliptic	underslung at rear	underslung at rear
underslung at rear	8' 7" short 10' 0" long	8' 7"
10' 0"	4' 4"	4' 4"
4' 4"	2/4 seater on short chassis (1934 - 36)	2 seater (1934 - 36)
open 4 seater (1933 - 34)	2 door saloon on long chassis (1934 - 36)	
	4 seater on long chassis (1934 - 36)	

TECHNICAL SPECIFICATIONS OF 2 LITRE PRODUCTION

MODELS 1936 - 1939

	15/98	15/98 Speed Model	15/98 Short Chassis	C - Type Speed Model
Approx. production or catalogue period	1936 - 1939	1936 - 1938	1937 - 1939	1938 - 1939
Number of cylinders	4	4	4	4
Bore & stroke	78 x 102 mm	78 x 102 mm	78 x 102 mm	78 x 102 mm
Capacity	1495,57 cc	1495,57 cc	1495,57 cc	1495,57 cc
Lubrication system	wet sump	dry sump	wet sump	dry sump
Valve location	overhead	overhead	overhead	overhead
Camshaft	single overhead	single overhead	single overhead	single overhead
Advertised power output		100 bhp plus at 5500 rpm		110 bhp at 5250 rpm
Clutch	Borg & Beck	Borg & Beck	Borg & Beck	Borg & Beck
Gearbox	unit 4-speed	unit 4-speed	unit 4-speed	unit 4-speed
Final drive	spiral bevel	spiral bevel	spiral bevel	spiral bevel
Brakes	4 wheel Girling	4 wheel Lockheed	4 wheel Girling	4 wheel Lockheed
Suspension	semi-elliptic	semi-elliptic	semi-elliptic	semi-elliptic
Chassis frame	underslung at rear	underslung at rear	underslung at rear	underslung at rear
Wheelbase	9' 8"	8' 6"	8' 3"	8' 6"
Track	4' 6½"	4' 6½"	4' 6½"	4' 6½"
Catalogued coachwork	4 door saloon (1936 - 39) 4 seater tourer (1936 - 39)	2 seater (1937 - 38)	2/4 seater (1937 - 39) drophead coupe (1937 - 39)	streamlined 2 seater (1938 - 39)

APPENDIX II

THE OWNERS CLUB

A BRIEF HISTORY BY ALAN ARCHER

The Club owes its origin to Mortimer Morris-Goodall, 'Mort' to so many sporting motorists. Having been fired with enthusiasm by an *International* bought when a brash lad of some 20 summers, and by his first meeting with A.C. ('Bert') Bertelli shortly after, his success led to the purchase of the team car LM7 and an invitation to drive under works control at Le Mans in 1933. His reverence for 'Bert and his Astons ... prompted the thought that almost everyone else who had the good fortune or sense to own one felt the same ... how nice it would be to meet some of the people'. S.C.H. ('Sammy') Davis agreed that the Aston Martin Owners Club would be a good idea and inserted a note in *Autocar* (of which he was Sports Editor) calling a meeting. The 20 or 30 people who turned up also agreed and elected a committee which included Lance Prideaux-Brune, Dick Anthony, Maurice Falkner, Harold Bevan, Miss Dorothy Bean and Peter Cadbury. Charles Jarrott was persuaded to become the President and Sammy Davis the Vice-President with Leslie Keevil as Honorary Treasurer and Mort Goodall as Honorary Secretary. The Club's activities, mostly social and including an annual dinner-dance at the Park Lane Hotel, were brought to a close by the Second World War.

Almost ten years later, in 1948, the late Dick Stallebrass and the late Dudley Coram started the process all over again and the Club was reformed. Although the pre-war archives of the Club have been missing for many years, the substance of the present rules is believed to enshrine the same principles as those drafted in 1935. They provide, *inter alia*, that the Club is established to 'promote the sport and pastime of motoring ...' and 'to develop interest in the ASTON MARTIN CAR ...'. In 1948 there was little

The Aston Martin Owners Club was formed in 1935 by that great enthusiast for the marque, Mortimer Morris-Goodall seen here (centre) with team mates D.M. Campbell and the late 'Dick' Anthony after winning the LCC Relay Race at Brooklands in 1936. Goodall's Le Mans model carries the original Club badge on the radiator.

hint of the further fame that would be earned in the years to come to add to the historic status of the Aston Martin as one of the world's great marques.

From the small groups that met in 1935 and 1948, the Club has grown steadily to become one of the foremost one-make clubs with worldwide membership. The pre-war social events and the first St. John Horsfall meeting at Silverstone have been followed by many different events all over the world, enabling enthusiasts to meet 'some of these people' almost anywhere in the world, from Australia to Stockholm, St. Lucia to Tokyo and in many of the United States of America. Thus does the Club cater for the devotees of an outstanding car which celebrated its Golden Jubilee in 1970 and continues to flourish today.

We are indebted to Alan Archer and the Aston Martin Owners Club for permission to re-print the above article which first appeared in their Club Register of summer 1976. All communications to the Club should be addressed to:
The Secretary, Mrs M. Hopkins, 293 Osbourne Road, Hornchurch, Essex.